TOURISM INDUSTRY IN NEW WORLD ORDER—FOCUS ON HOSPITALITY MANAGEMENT

Tourism Industry in New World Order—Focus on Hospitality Management

By

P.K. Bal

2008

CYBER TECH PUBLICATIONS
4264/3, Ansari Road, Daryaganj, New Delhi-110002 (India)
Ph.: 011-23244078. Fax: 011-23280028
E-Mail: cyberpublicationsdelhi@yahoo.com

**TOURISM INDUSTRY IN NEW WORLD ORDER—
FOCUS ON HOSPITALITY MANAGEMENT**

P.K. Bal

First Edition 2008

Published by :

G.S. Rawat for Cyber Tech Publications
4264/3, Ansari Road, Daryaganj, New Delhi-110002 (India)
Ph.: 011-23244078. Fax: 011-23280028
E-Mail: cyberpublicationsdelhi@yahoo.com

Preface

Tourism is one of the world's most rapidly growing industries and it has emerged as a fast growing sector in terms of employment and income generation. Hotels are complementary to it. Business of both depends on each other and hence are taken as same industry. Its contribution to the world economy is very significant. World Travel and Tourism Council has identified tourism as the world's most rapidly developing industry and its contribution to the world economy has almost doubled from 1990s. Besides employment generation, tourism sector has played a pivotal role in poverty alleviation and sustainable human development.

Against this background this collection of papers contributed by renowned writers, academicians and experienced administrators in the field of hospitality management embodies critical analysis of various aspects of tourism industry, both in theoretical and practical terms and makes concrete suggestions for revamping the tourism and hotel industry in India. The book examines the global, national and regional evolution of tourism sector, unfolds the recent issues and facets in tourism viz., geographical information system, strategic management, health, marketing strategies, sustainable development, service quality, personalization, natural environment, eco tourism and the impact of terrorism on tourism industry and a few micro level studies from an experimental perspective.

The views and opinions expressed by the contributors are of immense value for policy makers, planners, administrators and academicians for restructuring and rejuvenating policies and strategies related to tourism issues in the days to come.

Hope that this book will give you deeper insight into the real picture of the hospitality industry.

—*Author*

Contents

1

Hospitality Industry: An Introduction

HOTEL

A hotel is an establishment that provides paid lodging, usually on a short-term basis. Hotels often provide a number of additional guest services such as a restaurant, a swimming pool or childcare. Some hotels have conference services and meeting rooms and encourage groups to hold conventions and meetings at their location.

In Australia, the word may also refer to a pub or bar. In the UK similarly, many pubs with "hotel" in their name do not offer accommodation or even food.

In India, the word may also refer to a restaurant since the best restaurants were always situated next to a good hotel.

ORIGINS OF THE TERM

The word hotel derives from the French hotel, which referred to a French version of a townhouse or any other building seeing frequent visitors, not a place offering accommodation (in contemporary usage, hotel has the meaning of "hotel", and hotel particular is used for the old meaning). The French spelling (with the circumflex) was once also used in English, but is now rare. The circumflex replaces the 's' once preceding the 't' in the earlier hostel spelling, which over time received a new, but closely related meaning.

SERVICES AND FACILITIES

Basic accommodation of a room with only a bed, a cupboard, a small table and a washstand has largely been replaced by rooms with en-suite bathrooms and, more commonly in the United States than elsewhere, climate control. Other features found may be a telephone, an alarm clock, a TV, and broadband Internet connectivity. Food and drink may be supplied by a mini-bar (which often includes a small refrigerator) containing snacks and drinks (to be paid for on departure), and tea and coffee making facilities (cups, spoons, an electric kettle and sachets containing instant coffee, tea bags, sugar, and creamer or milk).

Some hotels offer various combinations of meals as part of a room and board arrangement. These are often advertised as:

European Plan	no meals are included, or only a minimal breakfast
American Plan	all meals included (full board)
Modified American Plan	option of breakfasts and dinners

In the United Kingdom a hotel is required by law to serve food and drinks to all comers within certain stated hours; to avoid this requirement it is not uncommon to come across "private hotels" which are not subject to this requirement.

However, in Japan the capsule hotel supplies minimal facilities and room space.

CLASSIFICATION

The cost and quality of hotels are usually indicative of the range and type of services available. Due to the enormous increase in tourism worldwide during the last decades of the 20th century, standards, especially those of smaller establishments, have improved considerably. For the sake of greater comparability, rating systems have been introduced, with the one to five stars classification being most common.

Boutique Hotels

"Boutique Hotel" is a term originating in North America to describe intimate, usually luxurious or quirky hotel environments. Boutique hotels differentiate themselves from larger chain or branded hotels by providing an exceptional and personalized level of accommodation, services and facilities.

Boutique hotels are furnished in a themed, stylish and/ or aspirational manner. Although usually considerably smaller than a mainstream hotel (ranging from 3 to 100 guest rooms) boutique hotels are generally fitted with telephone and wi-fi Internet connections, honesty bars and often cable/pay TV. Guest services are attended to by 24 hour hotel staff. Many boutique hotels have on site dining facilities, and the majority offer bars and lounges which may also be open to the general public.

Of the total travel market a small percentage are discerning travellers, who place a high importance on privacy, luxury and service delivery. As this market is typically corporate travellers, the market segment is non-seasonal, high-yielding and repeat, and therefore one which boutique hotel operators target as their primary source of income.

Motels

There is no hard and fast rule differentiating motels from other hotels, although a motel is clearly suggesting that it is aimed at motorists. This may simply mean that it is a hotel with good access to the road network (on a motorway or ring road) so that a long car journey need not be interrupted for long by town-centre traffic. In other cases the designation is simply an attempt to make the most of a poor location inconvenient for town-centre services and attractions. Classically, though, a motel is a hotel which is made convenient for people who, for whatever personal reason, wish to be able to have quick access from the outside world (especially from their parked car) to the hotel room-without passing the scrutiny of a receptionist or fellow guests. This is usually arranged by having rooms (sometimes in individual chalets or even trailers) arranged around the car park with room doors opening directly to the outside rather than to an internal corridor.

HISTORIC HOTELS

Some hotels have gained their renown through tradition, by hosting significant events or persons, such as Schloss Cecilienhof in Potsdam, Germany, which derives its fame from the so-called Potsdam Conference of the World War II allies Winston Churchill, Harry Truman and Joseph Stalin in 1945. Other establishments have given name to a particular meal or beverage, as is the case with the Waldorf Astoria in New York City, USA, known for its Waldorf Salad or the Raffles Hotel in Singapore, where the drink Singapore Sling was invented. Another example is the Hotel Sacher in Vienna Austria, home of the Sachertorte.

There are also hotels which became much more popular through films like the Grand Hotel Europe in Saint Petersburg, Russia when James Bond stayed there in the blockbuster Goldeneye. Cannes hotels such as the Carlton or the Martinez become the center of the world during Cannes Film Festival (France). A number of hotels have entered the public consciousness through popular culture, such as the Ritz Hotel in London, UK ('Putting on The Ritz') and Hotel Chelsea in New York City, subject of a number of songs and also the scene of the stabbing of Nancy Spungen (allegedly by her boyfriend Sid Vicious). Hotels that enter folklore like these two are also often frequented by celebrities, as is the case both with the Ritz and the Chelsea.

Unusual Hotels

Many hotels can be considered destinations in themselves, by dint of unusual features of the lodging and/or its immediate environment:

Treehouse Hotels

Some hotels, such as the Costa Rica Tree House in the Gandoca-Manzanillo Wildlife Refuge, Costa Rica, or Treetops Hotel in Aberdare National Park, Kenya, are built with living trees as structural elements, making them treehouses.

The Ariau Towers near Manaus, Brazil is in the middle of the Amazon, on the Rio Negro. Bill Gates even invested and had a suite built there with satellite internet/phone. Another hotel with treehouse units is Bayram's Tree Houses in Olympos, Turkey.

Cave Hotels

Desert Cave Hotel in Coober Pedy, South Australia and the Cuevas Pedro Antonio de Alarcón (named after the author) in Guadix, Spain, as well as several hotels in Cappadocia, Turkey, are notable for being built into natural cave formations, some with rooms underground.

Capsule Hotels

Capsule hotels are a type of economical hotels that are quite common in Japan.

Ice Hotels

Ice hotels, such as the Ice Hotel in Jukkasjarvi, Sweden, melt every spring and are rebuilt out of ice and snow each winter.

Snow Hotels

The Mammut Snow Hotel in Finland is located within the walls of the Kemi snow castle, which is the biggest in the world. It includes The Mammut Snow Hotel, The Castle Courtyard, The Snow Restaurant and a chapel for weddings, etc. Its furnishings and decorations, such as sculptures, are all made of snow and ice. A hotel which offers similar accommodation is the Lainio Snow Hotel in Lapland, near Ylläs, Finland.

Garden Hotels

Garden hotels, famous for their gardens before they became hotels, includes Gravetye Manor, the home of William Robinson and Cliveden, designed by Charles Barry with a rose garden by Geoffrey Jellicoe.

Underwater Hotels

As of 2005, the only hotel with an underwater room that can be reached without Scuba diving is Utter Inn in Lake Mälaren, Sweden. It only has one room, however, and Jules Undersea Lodge in Key Largo, Florida, which requires Scuba diving, is not much bigger.

Hydropolis is an ambitious project to build a luxury hotel in Dubai, UAE, with 220 suites, all on the bottom of the Persian Gulf, 20 meters (66 feet) below the surface. Its architecture will feature two domes that break the surface and an underwater train tunnel, all made of transparent materials such as glass and acrylic.

Other unusual Hotels

The Dariush Grand Hotel in Kish Island, Iran, built with the theme of the world heritage Persepolis.

The Library Hotel in New York City is unique in that its ten floors are arranged according to the Dewey Decimal System.

The Rogers Centre, formerly Sky Dome, in Toronto, Canada is the only stadium to have a hotel connected to it, with 70 rooms overlooking the field. West Ham United F.C.in the UK now has a hotel with rooms that overlook the pitch and sometimes double as executive boxes for important games.

The Burj al-Arab hotel in Dubai, United Arab Emirates, built on an artificial island, is structured in the shape of a sail of a boat. The RMS Queen Mary in Long Beach, California is the only 1930s ocean liner still in existence. Its elegant first-class staterooms are now used as a hotel.

The Oriental Pearl Tower in Shanghai houses an extremely expensive hotel with only 20 rooms.

WORLD-RECORD SETTING HOTELS

Tallest

The tallest hotel in the world is thought to be the Burj al-Arab in Dubai, United Arab Emirates, at 280 metres, which however will soon be surpassed by the nearby Rose Rotana Suites at 333 meters (1,091 feet). The Ryugyong Hotel in Pyongyang was intended to reach 330 meters (1,083 feet), but is unlikely to be completed; it has been under construction since 1987 and was abandoned in 1992. The Baiyoke Sky Hotel in Bangkok, Thailand has a building height of 309 meters, but rooms do not go all the way to the top.

The highest hotel rooms are in the Grand Hyatt in the Jin Mao Building in Shanghai, the highest floor being at around 350 m.

Largest

The largest hotel in the world is the MGM Grand Las Vegas in Las Vegas, Nevada, USA with a total of 6,276 rooms as of December 20, 2006. On December 18, 2006 Guinness World Records listed the First World Hotel in Genting Highlands, Malaysia as the world's largest hotel. It has a total of 6,118 rooms and is part of the Genting Highlands Resort and Casino. The First World Plaza which is joined to the two hotel towers boasts 500,000 square feet of indoor theme park, shopping centres, casino gaming areas, and eateries. Previously, Guinness had listed the MGM Grand Las Vegas in Las Vegas, Nevada, USA with 5,005 rooms as the largest hotel in the world.

In the past, other hotels have held the title of largest hotel in the world, in terms of the number of rooms. Some of these include the Rossiya Hotel near Moscow's Red Square, and the Ambassador City Jomtien in Pattaya, Thailand. Other large hotels being considered for development that may one day take the title are in Penang, Malaysia and Macau.

Oldest

According to the Guinness Book of World Records, the oldest hotel still in operation is the Hoshi Ryokan, in Awazu, Japan. It opened in 717, and features hot springs.

HOTEL OCCUPATIONS

The owner, chairman, or CEO of a hotel or hotel group is known as a hotelier. The front desk, housekeeping, security, valet parking, restaurant, accounting department, and sales and marketing are common departments of a mid or large sized hotel. The night auditor role falls within the front desk department but also carries some of the responsibilities of the accounting department.

The engineering staff takes care of building repairs and up keep of HVAC systems, plumbing, fire sprinkler systems, chillers, cooling towers, pool and spa if applicable, lights, breakers, door locks, C.P.R., laundry machines, kitchen walk ins, ice machines, building air handlers, room repairs and upkeep.

HOTEL CHAINS

A hotel chain is a collection or grouping of hotels under one recognizable brand operated by a management company. Best Western International claims to be the largest hotel chain in the world, in terms of the number of properties.

Living in the Hotels

A Few Examples

The American billionaire Howard Hughes lived much of his life in hotels. He moved with his entourage from hotel to hotel and from Beverly Hills to Boston before deciding to move to Las Vegas and become a casino baron. Less than a month after his November 27, 1966 arrival, Hughes made a public offer to buy the Desert Inn. The hotel's 8th floor became the nerve center of his empire and the 9th floor penthouse became Hughes' personal residence. Hughes moved to the Bahamas, Vancouver, London and several other locations-always taking up residence in the top floor penthouse of the hotel. Between 1966 and 1968, he also purchased several other hotel-casinos from the Mafia: Castaways, New Frontier, The Landmark Hotel and Casino, Sands and Silver Slipper.

Coco Channel made the Hotel Ritz in Paris her home for more than thirty years, until the day of her death, at 87, in a suite now named "Coco Chanel Suite".

King Peter II of Yugoslavia spent much of the Second World War at Claridge's, a hotel in London. His son, Aleksandar Karadordevic, was born in the hotel.

Prince Felix Yusupov lived in the Hotel Melia Vendome Paris in Paris.

Sultan Said Bin Taimur of Muscat lived at Dorchester Hotel in London after he was deposed by Qaboos of Oman in 1970, he died in the hotel in 1972.

Eleftherios Venizelos, Greek statesman and diplomat, lived in the Hotel Ritz Paris while he was in exile in France from 1935-1936.

Actress Elaine Stritch lives at the Carlyle Hotel in New York City. Magician Criss Angel lives at the Luxor Hotel in Las Vegas, Nevada. As of late 2006-present in the Presidential suite.

Hotels in Fiction

Hotels have been chosen by authors as settings for crime fiction, farce and mystery works. A hotel is perfect as a mysterious, anonymous setting where various characters may gather. Hotels also feature in films, television series, songs and even theme park rides.

Examples:

- Hyperion Hotel
- Grand Hotel
- Room Service
- The Hotel New Hampshire
- Fawlty Towers
- Four Rooms
- White Horse Inn
- Hotelier
- Hotel Babylon
- Hotel California
- Agatha Christie's Evil Under the Sun
- Hotel Denouement from the Penultimate Peril by Lemony Snicket
- Hotel Dolphin
- A Caribbean Mystery
- At Bertram's Hotel
- Cyril Hare's Suicide Excepted
- Hotel Rwanda is the name of a movie that involves a real hotel, Hotel des Mille Collines, in Rwanda where real events portrayed in the movie took place
- Hollywood Tower Hotel (ride at Disney-MGM Studios, Orlando, Florida)
- The Overlook Hotel from The Shining
- Hotel
- Hotel Trianon in Graham Greene's The Comedians
- The Leaky Cauldron

- Hotel Dusk
- The television series Las Vegas is set at the fictional Montecito Resort and Casino
- Crossroads Motel, later Kings Oak Country Hotel and Crossroads Hotel from the former British soap opera Crossroads
- The Tipton Hotel from the Disney Channel series "The Suite Life of Zack & Cody"

Hotel Rooms as an Investment

Some hotels sell individual rooms to investors. The buyer is allowed to stay in the room without charge or at a reduced rate for a given number of days each year. The investor is paid a share of the takings for the room. Rooms can be sold on a leasehold basis, sometimes on a 999 year lease. Room owners are free to sell at any time.

2

TYPES OF HOTELS

APARTMENT HOTEL

An Apartment Hotel (also ApartHotel, Apart Hotel and Apart-Hotel) is a type of accommodation, described as "a serviced apartment complex that uses a hotel style booking system". It is similar to renting an apartment, but with no fixed contracts and occupants can 'check-out' whenever they wish.

Apartment hotels are flexible types of accommodation; instead of the rigid format of a hotel room an apartment hotel complex usually offers a complete fully fitted apartment. These complexes are usually custom built, and similar to a hotel complex containing a varied amount of apartments. The length of stay in these apartment hotels is very varied with anywhere from a few days to months or even years. Prices tend to be cheaper than hotels. The people that stay in apartment hotels use them as a home away from home, therefore they are usually fitted with everything the average home would require.

ORIGIN

Apartment hotels were first created in holiday destinations as accommodation for families that needed to 'live' in an apartment rather than 'stay' as they would in a hotel. The apartments would provide a 'holiday home' but generally be serviced. Later on these apartments evolved to be complete homes, allowing occupants to do everything they would at home, such as cleaning, washing and cooking.

Services and Facilities

Essentially the apartment hotel combines the flexibility of apartment living with the service of a hotel. Many of the apartments take advantage of prime locations with panoramic views of cities seen through wall to ceiling windows. Suites usually include high quality finishes, broadband connection & interactive TV, servicing and integrated kitchen and bathroom. High quality leather sofas in the living area and king size beds bring the hotel experience to a whole new level. Those are the luxuries, they also come with the basics: satellite or cable TV, washer, dryer, dishwasher, cooker, oven, fridge, freezer, sink, shower, bath, wardrobes, all the furnishings to be expected in a luxury home.

EXTENDED STAY HOTELS

Extended stay hotels are a type of lodging with features unavailable at standard hotels. These features are intended to provide more home-like amenities. There are currently 27 extended stay chains in North America with at least 7 hotels, representing over 2,000 properties. There is substantial variation among extended stay hotels with respect to quality and the amenities that are available. Some of the economy chains attract clientele who use the hotels as semi-permanent lodging.

Extended-stay hotels typically have self-serve laundry facilities and offer discounts for extended stays, beginning at 5 or 7 days. They also have guestrooms (or "suites") with kitchens. The kitchens include at a minimum usually: a sink, a refrigerator (usually full size), a microwave oven, and a stovetop. Some kitchens also have dishwashers and conventional ovens.

Extended stay hotels are popular with business travellers on extended assignments, families in the midst of a relocation, and anyone else in need of temporary housing. Extended stay hotels are also used by travellers who appreciate the larger space a typical suite provides.

Residence Inn is credited with popularizing the "extended stay" concept. The chain was launched in 1975 in Wichita, Kansas by Jack DeBoer, and acquired by Marriott Corporation in 1987. As of April 2005, there were over 450 Residence Inn hotels in the United States, Canada and Mexico. Jack DeBoer has jumped back in the Extended Stay market developing a concept called Value Place.

One of today's most popular long term lodging brands came from the merger of Extended Stay America and Homestead Hotels. Both these chains were already well established when they combined in 2004 to become Extended Stay Hotels with over 670 owned and operated properties nationwide.

Another worldwide hotel chain, Choice Hotels International, franchisor for name brands such as Comfort Inn, Comfort Suites, Sleep Inn and Quality Inn, entered the extended stay market with their MainStay Suites brand. They proceeded to acquire the Suburban Extended Stay hotel chain in 2005, making them a sizeable extended stay system with over 150 hotels open and under development.

Hospitality Service

The concept of Hospitality Services, also known as "accommodation sharing", "hospitality exchange", and "home stay networks", refers to centrally organized social networks of individuals who trade accommodation without monetary exchange. While this concept could also include house swapping or even time share plans, it has come to be associated mostly with travellers and tourists staying with one another free of charge. Since the 1990s, these services have increasingly moved away from using printed catalogues and phone trees to connect users towards Internet websites. These have grown exponentially since 2000 and as of March, 2007 over 500,000 people are registered users of these networks. These vary in operational structure, place different emphasis on graphical vs. textual formatting, and cater disproportionately to specific geographic regions.

History

In 1949, Bob Luitweiler founded the first hospitality service called Servas Open Doors as a cross national, non-profit, volunteer run organization advocating interracial and international peace. The next earliest began in 1965 when John Wilcock set up the Traveler's Directory, originally as a listing of his mutual friends willing to host each other when travelling. This later became the Hospitality Exchange in 1988 when Joy Lily rescued the organization from imminent demise. Hospitality Club is the direct successor Hospex, the first Internet-based service, operating out of Germany since 1992. It is currently the largest hospitality exchange network, and is growing exponentially. CouchSurfing is a newer but also rapidly growing hospitality exchange organization founded in 2004. Just as all the individual services have their own individual creation stories and organizational histories (often including demise and resurrection), many also have specific niche markets that they cater to including students, activists, religious pilgrims, and even occupational groups like police officers. However, the trend in recent years points to a greater consolidation of users in networks without a specific group, value, or lifestyle affiliation.

How they Work

In essence, these systems employ reciprocity-users gain access to other users' information only by posting their own. Required fields normally include name and contact information, though newer services encourage users to include more detailed personal material, including likes and dislikes, hopes and dreams, and even photographs. Of course, more information included tends to improve the chances that someone will find them trustworthy enough to host or stay with while travelling. It is very much akin to on-line dating services.

BENEFITS

Monetary Savings

Staying in private homes means that travellers can save lots of money on accommodation that they would usually be spending on hotels or hostels. Used over a long period of time (2 to 4 weeks), this strategy can cut overall travel budgets in half, or even more combined with hitchhiking. These savings can then be passed on towards more generously patronizing local establishments or simply staying abroad for longer periods of time.

Local Economic Sustainability

Many tourist vacations today are sold in package form, often including flights, hotels, rental cars, sightseeing tours, and coupons for chain restaurants and bars. While this makes purchasing more convenient, it also puts more money in the hands of large multinational corporations exploiting the synergy strategy of marketing their products in the context of their subsidiary companies operating in other markets. Many years ago, this might have been termed collusion; today, however, it is the norm. This comes at the expense of locally owned independent businesses. Accommodation sharing helps to break apart this monopoly and hopefully redirects some of the tourist revenue back to the local or national economy.

Ecological Sustainability

While this is especially important in more rural travel venues where hotels are often built in very picturesque, though fragile environments, every night stayed at a local's home means that much less demand for such hotel rooms. Also, if accommodation sharing does in fact increase the length of average stays, it may reduce the amount of trips to and from different locations and back home again, thus reducing the overall fuel expenditures in the process.

Local Contact

Ostensibly, one of the primary reasons we travel is to experience what life is like for people living in other countries. Making interpersonal connections and fostering understanding of different cultures may in the long run also be important to international relations. However, even in our increasingly globalized world supposedly rife with diversity, in many popular travel destinations we find tourists milling around "tourist enclaves" where the companies they patronize back home have set up shop to cater to their desires while they are abroad. Sociologist George Ritzer has referred to this phenomenon as the "McDonaldisation of society" and the more recently, the "globalization of nothing". The location of hotels near these centers only fosters more convenient envelopment of the tourist dollar. During hospitality exchanges, hosts want to show off their local knowledge and exciting "off the map" venues. Not only may travellers get a distinctly different experience, but they will also get a feel for the everyday lives of local residents.

Reciprocity

These systems foster richer and more convenient travel experiences not so much on the premise of altruism, but on the basis of social exchange theory. Implicit in the agreement to host travellers is the ability to ask to be hosted by them in the future. If one enjoys having interesting guests in their home, this works out well for both parties. It works comparatively better if you are visited by travellers from a locale you find particularly attractive. Thus, hosting someone from New York City in Gainesville, FL seems to be an unbelievable opportunity. Moreover, if you are a Westerner visiting someone in a developing nation, your stay might be the only way that this individual or family could afford a trip to a rich nation. This may mean more than just a relaxing vacation for such disadvantaged parties.

Authenticity and Adventure

Tourism has always searched for these two qualities, but much like Midas and his golden touch, the reach of tourism has to a large extent destroyed the opportunity to encounter them in most places. Unluckily, the experience has been thoroughly commodified by everyone who wanted to secure their opportunity to make a buck in the process. Accommodation sharing offers a way out of this bind and a viable alternative to having one's desires manipulated by corporate conglomerates who never had the best interests of the place or the people foremost in their minds.

DRAWBACKS

Lack of Guarantee

There is no contractual agreement between users in these systems. Reservations are made, but if they are for some reason broken, there is no higher authority to which one could plead for a refund or other compensation. The only repercussion will be the poor rating you give that user and your only consolation will be that your warning will deter others from visiting or hosting them. For those who feel insecure unless their travel arrangements are written in stone before departure, this system will not be comforting.

Potential Interpersonal Conflict or Awkwardness

There is a chance that guest and host will not get along. Perhaps there will be scheduling or ideological conflicts. Maybe you will find that hosts or visitors have misrepresented themselves. Perhaps the experience will not live up to your expectations. Intense interpersonal communications in advance and a flexibility once you have arrived is your best bet. These experiences require additional planning and courtesy towards the demands of your host. Thus, your living conditions, length of stay, and overall experience will be circumscribed by the living conditions you enter into.

Digital Divide and Demographic Segregation

The average user is a young white person who speaks English and lives in a developed nation. While there are many users who do not fit this description, the more different they are, the less likely they will be involved. This is especially true for persons living in the developing world who likely do not have easy access to the fundamental prerequisite for using these services: computers and the Internet. Thus, the sample population found in searches of these databases are really much less diverse than a geographical representation of worldwide users might suggest.

Security

There is a distinct possibility that someone will abuse the system and that innocent users (especially women) will get hurt. All services include disclaimers that require users to waive their rights to hold anyone but themselves responsible for any harm that may come to them in using the system. They advise that the best defense mechanism is to only involve oneself with users that have extensive personal information and interpersonal networks within the system that have been verified by others. It does seem entirely plausible that someone clever and patient enough might be able to invent an entire group of complex user identities and build histories convincing enough to fool even more cautious patrons. Still, the difference between these systems and the other social networking platforms popular nowadays on the web (such as MySpace, Tribe, Orkut, LiveJournal and Ebay) is that any agreement reached through the accommodation sharing medium is contingent on actually meeting other people face-to-face. Other web scams are easier because interpersonal interactions rely so much on putative identities that are never actually verified in the real world. However, this does not diminish the greater risk to physical well being that this kind of travelling by definition must entertain. The best advice is to meet unknown persons in public spaces first, and try to meet some of their acquaintances in person before agreeing to a hospitality exchange.

COUCHSURFING

The CouchSurfing Project is a free international Internet-based hospitality service. As of April 2007, it had more than 208,000 members in 216 countries and territories. From various indicators it can be estimated that many members were actively using the website, with 40% offering their couches to host travellers (with another 22% saying "maybe" and others who are travelling at the moment).

Members use the website, initially designed by founder Casey Fenton, to coordinate accommodations. It features extensive profiles, and uses an optional credit card verification system, a personal vouching system, and personal references to increase security and trust. There are many other features on the site, such as interest discussion groups, meeting functionality, live chat and more.

In June 2006 the project experienced a number of computer problems resulting in much of the database being lost. It was initially announced that the project was being ended; however, within days it was confirmed that the site would be rebuilt, and users were again able to login (but not yet access the site's full functions). "CouchSurfing 2.0" was announced on 3 July 2006, planned to be operational within 10 days.

As of July 7th 2006 couchsurfing.com is once again fully operational although some, mostly inactive profiles, group postings and personal messages seem to have been lost. Most functions and pages are unchanged (the biggest change is the way friend links are managed now) and the site is called "2.0" now because of a philosophical change, the site's motto is "Participate in Creating a Better World, One Couch

At A Time". In August a CS wiki was launched where everyone is invited to participate and make CouchSurfing better.

Organization

CouchSurfing International Inc. is a Not-for-profit corporation incorporated in the US state of New Hampshire, created on 4/2/2003. Until July 2004 CouchSurfing reported itself to be a non-profit registered according to section 501(c)(3) of the United States Internal Revenue Code. Casey Fenton stated that on 27 January 2007 that CouchSurfing is not a registered 501(c) non-profit and is currently run by a board of which he is the only member, until the process of moving to 501(c)(3) is completed.

The mission statement of CouchSurfing is Participate in Creating a Better World, One Couch at a Time: "CouchSurfing seeks to internationally network people and places, create educational exchanges, raise collective consciousness, spread tolerance and facilitate cultural understanding. As a community we strive to do our individual and collective parts to create a better world, and we believe that the surfing of couches is a means to accomplish this goal. CouchSurfing is not about the furniture, not just about finding free accommodations around the world; it's about making connections worldwide. We make the world a better place by opening our homes, our hearts, and our lives. We open our minds and welcome the knowledge that cultural exchange makes available. We create deep and meaningful connections that cross oceans, continents and cultures. CouchSurfing wants to change not only the way we travel, but how we relate to the world!"

Couchsurfing.com is registered by Casey Fenton Consulting. CouchSurfing.org points to the same website as CouchSurfing.com, though there are some other websites using similar addresses, such as couchsurfing.net, the German couchsurfing.de, and couchsurfing.info (which points to a forum on Hospitality Club), and opencouchsurfing.org.

Finances

CouchSurfing claims that "the founders and admins are volunteers". Their 2005 Summary of Expenses though shows that 62% of the donations in 2005 have been used for the payroll and travel expenses against only 24% on IT expenses. In 2005 CouchSurfing paid a total of US$13,500 in payroll.

How it Works

Membership in the organization is free and is obtained simply by registering on the website. The core activity of the organization is exchange of accommodation. Acting as a host, a member offers the possibility of accommodation at his or her leisure; it is not required, but obviously it is encouraged. Acting as a surfer (guest), a traveller may search for and request accommodation at his or her destination. Accommodation is entirely consensual between the host and surfer, and the duration, nature, and terms of the surfer's stay are generally worked out in advance to the convenience of both parties. It is also expected to be free; no monetary exchange takes place except under certain circumstances (e.g. the surfer may compensate the host for food). There are three methods to ensure security and trust, which are all visible on member profiles for potential hosts and surfers to see prior to arranging anything with each other:

1. Personal references, which hosts and surfers could leave for each other at their option after having used the service.
2. An optional credit card verification system, which allowed members to "lock in" their name and address by making a credit card payment and entering a code that CouchSurfing mails to the billing address (this also allows CS to recuperate some costs by requiring a small donation for verification).
3. A personal vouching system, whereby a member that had been vouched for-originally starting with the

founders of the site-might in turn vouch for any number of other members he or she knew or had met through CouchSurfing, and trusts.

Volunteers within the project often arrange meetings or camps which are events that last several days and bring people together.

Since June 2006, the website has been run in large part by CouchSurfing Collectives, which are groups of CouchSurfers who get together in a chosen city to develop and improve CouchSurfing. The first three Collectives took place in Montreal, Vienna, and New Zealand.

Members who wish to volunteer for various tasks on the site and help spread the word about CouchSurfing in general may become ambassadors. Ambassadors must be verified and actively promote the CouchSurfing spirit among members and to the public. In addition to promoting use of the site, they greet new members, help with questions and other administrative tasks, and more, all on a volunteer basis.

Criticisms

During the "temporary failure" described below, CouchSurfing was criticised for making errors in backing up and then just letting the project die. The decision seemed to some to have been taken by one person only-founder Casey Fenton's initial announcement cited personal reasons and quoted guru Osho. In fact, the decision was made by a collective group of core volunteers and Admins that best understood the seriousness of the situation.

Temporary Failure of the Project

The CouchSurfing project was taken down temporarily due to a major database error on June 30, 2006.

An email sent by Fenton, to members of the project reported that a fatal database error had occurred-too much important data was lost to allow the project to continue in its current form. He decided to stop the project for personal reasons, but later changed his mind.

However, many members protested, offering assistance and donations, and within days it was confirmed that the site would be rebuilt. "CouchSurfing 2.0" was announced on 3 July 2006, planned to be operational within 10 days. As of July 7 the website was up again. Most of the profiles could be recovered, and CS claims that those that were lost were largely those of inactive members.

Immediately following the announcement of June 30, some websites started up in response, promoting attempts to help rebuild CouchSurfing; some sites request users to enter their CouchSurfing.com details. However, such sites were not officially endorsed, and members have been warned against giving their personal details to other sites. The Resort

INTRODUCTION

A resort is a place used for relaxation or recreation, attracting visitors for holidays or vacations. Resorts are places, towns such as Sochi in Russia, Newport, Rhode Island or St. Moritz, Switzerland, or larger regions, like the Adirondack Mountains or the Italian Riviera. A resort is not merely a commercial establishment operated by a single company, although in the late twentieth century this sort of facility became more common. Such a self-contained resort attempts to provide for all or most of a vacationer's wants while remaining on the premises, such as food, drink, lodging, sports, entertainment, and shopping.

The term "resort" sometimes is misused to identify a hotel that does not provide the other amenities required of a full resort. However, a hotel is frequently a central feature of a resort, such as the Grand Hotel at Mackinac Island, Michigan. Towns that contain resorts-or where tourism or vacationing is a major part of the local activity-are often called resort towns.

The Walt Disney World Resort is a prominent example of a modern, self-contained commercial resort. Resorts exist throughout the world, increasingly attracting visitors from around the globe. Thailand, for instance, has become a popular destination. Resorts are especially prevalent in Central America and the Caribbean.

Closely related to resorts are convention and large meeting sites. Generally these occur in cities where special meeting halls, together with ample accommodations as well as varied dining and entertainment are provided.

TYPES OF RESORT

Resort at a Destination

A commercial establishment at a resort destinaton such as a recreational area, a scenic or historic site, a theme park, a gaming facility or other tourist attraction competes with other businesses at that destination.. Examples would be hotels in and around Disney World, resorts in St. Martin in the Caribbean, and establishments at Aspen, Colorado in the USA.

Destination Resort

A destination resort is a resort that contains, in and of itself, the necessary guest attraction capabilities-that is to say that a destination resort does not need to be near a destination (town, historic site, theme park, or other) to attract its public.

Consequently, another characteristic of a destination resort is that is offers food, drink, lodging, sports, entertainment, and shopping within the facility so that guests have no need to leave the facility throughout their stay. Commonly these facilities are of higher quality than would be expected if one were to stay at a hotel or eat in a town's restaurants. Some examples are Atlantis in the Bahamas, Costa do Sauípe in the Northeastern Brazil, Laguna

Phuket in Thailand and Sun City near Johannesburg in South Africa.

All-inclusive Resort

An all-inclusive resort is a resort that, besides providing all of the common amenities of a resort, charges a fixed price that includes most or all items. At a minimum, most inclusive resorts include lodging, unlimited food, drink, sports activities, and entertainment for the fixed price. In recent years, the number of resorts offering "all-inclusive" amenities has decreased dramatically; in 1961, over half offered such plans and in 2007, less than ten percent do so.

HISTORICAL RESORTS

A famous resort of the ancient world was Baiae, Italy, popular over 2,000 years ago. Capri, an island near Naples, Italy, has attracted visitors since Roman times.

Another famous historical resort was Monte Ne, Arkansas, which was active in the early 20th century. At its peak more than 10,000 people a year visited its hotels. It was disenfranchised in the 1930s and flooded in the 1960s and all that remains are ruins.

CONDO-HOTEL

A condo-hotel, hotel-condo, or a Condotel is a building used as both a condominium and a hotel.

This type of residential building meets several needs that make it attractive. As development costs increase, the cost of hotel development can make developing new hotels difficult, especially in major cities. By selling the units as condos, the developer moves much of the development cost to the condo owners. By owning units that can be rented as hotel rooms, the owners are able to get a return on their investment allowing them the ability to own a residence in a resort or major city.

The U.S. Government is very strict about the type of advertising that can be done vis a vis Condo Hotel projects.

Some condo projects have advertised themselves as "Real Estate Investments"-since the value of these condos as a real estate investment is not entirely clear-the U.S. Government currently disallows use of this reference when advertising condo hotels.

Condo hotels have been criticized in California for allowing developers to skirt laws designed to protect public access to beaches. Because such a facility has hotel rooms, it can be classified as a public accommodation, even though the majority of the units are privately held, and the facility does little to accommodate the public.

While not intended as a complete list, the most popular locations in the U.S. for condo hotels include: Chicago, Miami, Fort Lauderdale, the Las Vegas metropolitan area, New York City, Myrtle Beach, South Carolina and Orlando, Florida.

MEGARESORT

A Megaresort, a type of destination resort, integrates the services offered by a hotel, casino, dining, entertainment, and shopping into a single, large, and highly stylized or themed venue. The hotels along the Las Vegas Strip are most typically thought of as megaresorts owing to their immense size and complexity.

The first megaresort is generally considered to have been The Mirage given its size and emphasis on non-gaming entertainment options like shopping and fine dining to draw in customers.

Megaresorts use the same fantastic or mythical theme (medieval life at Excalibur, tropical at The Mirage, famous cities, etc.) throughout their properties.

Megaresorts on the Las Vegas Strip

Listed from north to south:

Name	Rooms
Stratosphere	2,444
Wynn Las Vegas	2,716
Treasure Island (TI)	2,900
The Venetian	4,049
The Mirage	3,044
Harrah's	2,667
Caesars Palace	3,349
Bellagio	3,953
Paris	2,916
Planet Hollywood	2,567
Monte Carlo	3,014
MGM Grand	5,044
New York-New York	2,035
Excalibur	4,008
Luxor	4,476
Mandalay Bay (including the hotel)	4,825

SEASIDE RESORT

A seaside resort is a resort located on the coast. Where a beach is the primary focus for tourists, it may be called a beach resort.

History of the Seaside Resort

The coast has always been a recreational environment, although until the mid-nineteenth century, such recreation was a luxury only for the wealthy. Even in Roman times, the town of Baiae, by the Tyrrhenian Sea in Italy, was a resort for those who were sufficiently prosperous. During the early nineteenth century, the Prince Regent popularised Brighton, on the south coast of England, as a fashionable alternative to the wealthy spa towns such as Bath. Later, Queen Victoria's long-standing patronage of the Isle of Wight ensured the seaside residence was a highly fashionable possession for those wealthy enough to afford more than one home.

It was in the mid-nineteenth century that it became popular for people from less privileged classes to take holidays at seaside resorts. Improvements in transportation brought about by the industrial revolution enabled people to take holidays away from home, and led to the growth of coastal towns as seaside resorts. This is perhaps most strongly evidenced in England and Wales, country's shaped such that its coast is no more than 180 km from any point.

British Seaside Resorts

As the nineteenth century progressed, British working class day-trippers travelled on organised trips such as railway excursions, or by steamer, for which long piers were erected so that the ships bringing the trade could berth.

The popularisation of the seaside resort during this period was nowhere more pronounced than in Blackpool. Blackpool catered for workers from across industrial Northern England, who packed its beaches and promenade. Other northern towns (for example Scarborough, Bridlington and Skegness on the east coast) shared in the success of this new concept, which spread rapidly to other British coastal towns including several on the coast of North Wales and notably Rhyl, and Llandudno, the largest resort in Wales and known as "The Queen of the Welsh Resorts", a title first implied as early as 1864. Some resorts, such as Bournemouth, were built as new towns by local landowners to appeal to wealthier holidaymakers.

From the last quarter of the twentieth century, the popularity of the British seaside resort has declined for the same reason that it first flourished: advancements in transportation. The greater accessibility of foreign holiday destinations, through package holidays and, more recently, European low-cost airlines, affords people the freedom to holiday abroad. Despite the loyalty of returning holiday-makers, resorts such as Blackpool have struggled to compete against the favourable weather of Southern European alternatives. Now, many symbols of the traditional British resort (holiday camps, end-of-the-pier shows and saucy postcards) are regarded by some as drab and outdated; the skies are imagined to be overcast (although British summers from the late 1980s onwards have often been warmer and sunnier than at any other time in living memory) and the beach windswept.

In contrast, the fortunes of Brighton, which has neither holiday camps nor end-of-the-pier shows, have grown considerably, and, because of this, the resort is repeatedly held up as the model of a modern resort. However, unlike the Golden Miles of other British resorts, the sea is not Brighton's primary attraction: rather it is a backdrop against which is set an attitude of broad-minded cosmopolitan hedonism. The resulting sense of uniqueness has, coupled with the city's proximity to London, led to Brighton's restoration as a fashionable resort and the dwelling-place of the affluent.

Other English coastal towns have successfully sought to project a sense of their unique character. In particular, Southworld on the Suffolk coast is an active yet peaceful retirement haven with an emphasis on calmness, quiet countryside and jazz. Weymouth in Dorset offers itself as 'the gateway to the Jurassic Coast', Britain's only natural World Heritage Site. Newquay in Cornwall offers itself as the 'surfing capital of Britain', hosting international surfing events on its shores.

Torbay in South Devon is known is also known as The English Riviera. Consisting of the towns of Torquay, Paignton and Brixham, the bay has 20 beaches and coves along its 22 mile coastline, ranging from small secluded coves to the larger promenade style seafronts of Torquay's Torre Abbey Sands and Paignton Sands. Paignton Pier extends into the sea from the popular seafront.

IRISH SEASIDE RESORTS

Northern Ireland

Northern Ireland has a number of seaside resorts. The premier Northern Irish seaside resort is Portrush, often considered as the Northern Ireland's equivalent of Blackpool. Portrush is situated on the north coast of Northern Ireland as has two sandy beaches, a world-famous golf course Royal Portrush Golf Club, amusements, bars, nightclubs and restaurants. Newcastle is another seaside resort in Northern Ireland and is located on the east coast at the foot of the Mourne Mountains.

Other quieter and more scenic coastal towns are Ballycastle and Portstewart, both on the Northern Irish north coast.

Irish Riviera

The Irish Riviera features the pretty seaside resorts of Youghal, Ardmore, Dungarvan, Cobh and Ballycotton. These are a group of resort towns and villages all set close to the sunny south coast of Ireland. Each town has its own character with its own attractions, places to stay, places to eat, traditional Irish pubs and beauty spots. Youghal has been a favoured holiday destination for over 100 years and is right in the centre of the south coast of Ireland. The town is situated on the banks of the majestic Blackwater river as it reaches the sea. Youghal is well known for its beaches, being the only town in the Republic of Ireland with not one, but two, beaches that have been awarded EU Blue Flag status. Dungarvan is a thriving seaside market town nestled beneath the mountains in the centre of the Irish south coast.

Kinsale is often described as a food lovers and yachting town-a great base from which to explore the Irish Riviera. There is a very diverse range of restaurants and a vibrant nightlife. Kinsale is also home to a large and active creative community and there are numerous art galleries, record and book shops and several excellent delicatessens. Cobh is a perfect base for a wide variety of leisure and sport activities including fishing, sailing, windsurfing, canoeing, powerboating and of course walking and golf.

LUXURY RESORT

A luxury resort, sometimes referred to as an exclusive resort, is a very expensive vacation facility which is fully staffed and has been rated with five stars. Luxury resorts often boast many visitor activities and attractions such as golf, watersports, spa and beauty facilities, skiing, natural ecology and tranquillity. Because of the extent of amenities offered, a luxury resort is also considered a destination resort.

A luxury resort is an elite luxury property which exhibits an exceptionally high degree of customer service and hospitality. A flawless execution of guest services will be the resort staff's and management's main concern. A luxury resort will commonly also feature a superb architectural interior and exterior design as well as an interesting physical location.

The interior design will normally be elegant with stylish bedroom decor, exceptional dining facilities, and manicured landscaping and meticulous grounds. Luxury resorts will often also be in based in exceptionally desirable and strategic worldwide locations, from beautiful tropical islands, to snow caked mountains, to scenic lakes and rivers, to exhilarating cities. The locations will often be famous for featured activities from skiing to golf, water spots, diving, fishing, sailing and nature walks to glamorous shopping and nightlife entertainment.

A luxury resort may vary greatly in character, style and theme from resort to resort. A luxury resort will, however, normally be characterized by a high level of luxury, sophistication and, of course, price. Accommodations are first class, whether they follow a classic and traditional nature or a more minimalist and modern styling. An unmatched level of comfort will be available at a luxury resort, as well as many personalized services and amenities.

List of Resorts

Resorts with other than just skiing

Disney resorts are near the bottom

Individual non-casino resorts

- Angel Fire Resort
- Banana Bank
- Big Sky Resort
- Blue Harbor Resort
- Boca Raton Resort & Club
- Bodysgallen Hall
- Canaan Valley Resort State Park
- Calcot Manor
- Cacapon Resort State Park
- Celtic Manor Resort
- Claremont Resort
- Coeur d'Alene Resort
- Eagle Springs Golf Resort (9 holes)
- Fairfield Resorts
- Fontainebleau Resorts
- Grand Sierra Resort
- Grand Targhee Resort

- Grossinger's Catskill Resort Hotel
- Halltorps Manor
- Hedonism Resorts
- Hershey Entertainment and Resorts Company
- Hidden Valley Resort
- Hotel Buena Vista Beach Resort
- Kanwatheertha Beach Resort
- Kulu Bay Resort
- Lake Lawn Resort
- Legends Hotel and Resort
- McKinley Chalet Resort
- Mesilau Nature Resort
- Mirage Resorts
- Mont Tremblant Resort
- Moscow Country Club Resort
- Nemacolin resort
- Pinehurst Resort (golf)
- Poseidon resorts
- Primadonna Resorts
- Primm Valley Resort
- The Resort at Summerlin
- Resort World in Malaysia
- Resorts World in Singapore
- Rio Quente Resorts in Brazil
- Riverside Resort Hotel & Casino
- Ross Bridge Golf Resort and Spa
- San Luis Resort
- Sandy Lane (resort)

- Sani Resort in Greece
- Seaside resorts in Wales
- Starwood Hotels & Resorts Worldwide
- Stonewall Jackson Resort State Park
- Sunway Lagoon Resort Hotel
- Sycamore Mineral Springs Resort
- Tangalooma Wild Dolphin Resort
- Universal Orlando Resort
- Vail Resorts
- Westgate Resorts
- Wintergreen Resort
- Wynn Resorts
- Xanterra Parks and Resorts

Casino Resorts

- Atlantis Casino Resort
- Avi Resort & Casino
- Burswood Entertainment Complex
- Chukchansi Gold Resort & Casino
- French Lick Resort Casino
- Grand Sierra Resort
- Las Ramblas Resort-proposed
- Mandalay Resort Group
- MGM Mirage
- MontBleu Resort Casino & Spa
- Morongo Casino, Resort & Spa
- Niagara Fallsview Casino Resort
- Pechanga Resort and Casino
- Silver Legacy Resort Casino

- Sun Lakes Resort
- Tropicana Resort & Casino
- Trump Entertainment Resorts
- Turning Stone Casino & Resort

Chain Resorts

- Beaches Family Resorts (four resorts)
- Chandris Hotels and Resorts
- Club Med (many varied resorts world-wide)
- Destination Hotels & Resorts
- Fairmont Hotels and Resorts
- Hilton Hotels Corporation
- Hong Kong Resort Company
- Host Hotels & Resorts
- Marriott Hotels & Resorts
- Mövenpick Hotels & Resorts
- Outrigger Hotels & Resorts
- Princess (Hotels & Resorts) (Spain and nearby)
- Sandals Resorts (14 resorts in the Caribbean)
- Starwood Hotels & Resorts Worldwide
- Universal Parks & Resorts
- Wyndham Hotels & Resorts

Disney Resorts

- Disneyland Resort
- Disneyland Resort Paris
- Hong Kong Disneyland Resort (two hotels)
- Shanghai Disneyland Resort--under construction
- Tokyo Disney Resort

- Walt Disney World resorts (at Walt Disney World Resort)
    * Animal Kingdom Area Resorts
    * Epcot Area Resorts (six resorts)
    * Magic Kingdom Area Resorts

Shelved Disney Resorts

This section is unlikely to be complete

* Disney's America--never built
* Disney's Mineral King Ski Resort--never built
* Disney's Asian Resort--never built
* Disney's Mediterranean Resort--never built
* Disney's Persian Resort--never built
* Disney's Venetian Resort--never built

RESORT TOWN

The majority of shops in downtown Jackson, Wyoming cater to tourists. A resort town, sometimes called a resort destination, is a town or area where tourism or vacationing is a primary component of the local culture and economy. Most resort towns have one or more actual resorts in or nearby, although some places are considered resort towns merely because of their popularity among tourists.

Typically, the economy of a resort town is geared almost entirely towards catering to tourists, with most residents of the area working in the tourism or resort industry. Shops and luxury boutiques selling locally-themed souvenirs, motels, and unique restaurants often proliferate the downtown areas of a resort town.

Resort Town Economy

If the resorts or tourist attractions are seasonal in nature (such as a ski resort), resort towns typically experience a on-season where the town is bustling with tourists and workers, and an off-season where the town is populated only by a small amount of local year-round residents.

In addition, resort towns are often popular with wealthy retirees and people wishing to purchase vacation homes, which typically drives up property values and the cost of living in the region. Sometimes resort towns can become boomtowns due to the quick development of retirement and vacation-based residences.

However, most of the employment available in resort towns are typically low paying and it can be difficult for workers to afford to live the area in which they are employed. Many resort towns have spawned nearby bedroom communities where the majority of the resort workforce lives. Resorts towns sometimes struggle with problems regarding sustainable growth, due to the seasonal nature of the economy, the dependence on a single industry, and the difficulties in retaining a stable workforce.

EXAMPLES OF RESORT TOWNS

Asia

- Matheran, India

Middle East

- Dahab, Egypt
- Eilat, Israel

North America

Canada

- Whistler, British Columbia
- Banff, Alberta

United States

- Jackson, Wyoming

- Laughlin, Nevada
- Las Vegas Strip
- Vail, Colorado
- Aspen, Colorado
- Ruidoso, New Mexico
- Park City, Utah
- Ocean City, NJ
- Mackinaw City, MI

Europe

- Barizo, Spain
- Druskininkai, Lithuania
- Juodkrante, Lithuania
- Nida, Lithuania
- Palanga, Lithuania
- Varna, Bulgaria

BIDDING PROCESS

Marina Bay

In December 2004, the government of Singapore called for a request-for-concept (RFC), inviting industry players to submit concept proposals for the Integrated Resorts. A total of 19 bids were submitted during the RFC. Four companies/ consortiums placed their formal bids for the Marina Bay site, including:

- Genting International/Star Cruises
- Harrah's Entertainment/Keppel Land
- Las Vegas Sands
- MGM Mirage/CapitaLand

While Harrah's and MGM were considered forerunners, Las Vegas Sands emerged as the surprise winner when it was announced on 26 May 2006. The Marina Bay Sands is billed as a centrepiece of the Marina Bay landscape when completed in 2009. Las Vegas Sands had committed the highest development investment of S$3.85 billion. With the land price and associated capital cost, its total investment will exceed S$5 billion. It would also be one of the most expensive casinos in the world. The design, by Moshe Safdie consists of three large shells containing conference halls and other business venues, three large hotel towers linked on their top floors by a sweeping sky garden, and a centerpiece museum which juts out onto the bay.

"Sands has submitted the best overall proposal that meets our economic tourism objective. In particular, the proposal will significantly strengthen Singapore's position as a leading MICE destination and the proposal also possesses unique design elements that will provide a memorable image for Marina Bay." Singapore Deputy Prime Minister S. Jayakumar

Sentosa

Three consortiums submitted their proposals by the due date on 10 October 2006, including:

- Eighth Wonder with Publishing and Broadcasting Limited, Melco International Development Limited, Isle of Capri Casinos Inc. (Design by Peter Marino)
- Genting International with Star Cruises, Universal Studios (Design by Michael Graves)
- Kerzner International with Capitaland (Design by Frank Gehry)

A fourth contender, a Harrah's Entertainment and Keppel Land consortium pulled out from the race four days before the deadline.

The bids were reviewed by a ministerial committee and a tender evaluation committee. The ministerial committee was headed by Deputy Prime Minister Prof S Jayakumar and included Tharman Shanmugaratnam, S Iswaran, Mah

Bow Tan, Lim Hng Kiang, Dr Vivian Balakrishnan and Raymond Lim as its members.

Results were announced on 8 December 2006. The winning consortium was front-runner Genting International and Star Cruises with their bid for the Resorts World at Sentosa.

"Genting submitted the most compelling proposal overall that best meets our economic and tourism objectives. In particular, the proposal reflects our vision for the Sentosa IR as a large-scale, family resort with its host of world-class family leisure attractions and other strong offerings. The attractions will position Sentosa and draw a significant number of new and repeat visitors," DPM Prof S. Jayakumar.

SKI RESORT

A ski area is a developed recreational facility, usually on a mountain or large hill, containing ski trails and vital supporting services. It is common for a ski area to have food, rental equipment, parking facilities and a ski lift system catering to the sports of skiing and snowboarding. Normally located in high mountain areas (or at least on well-built-up hills) for optimum snow coverage, they have become ubiquitous in areas where skiing is a popular pastime. The paths are usually marked and known as runs, trails or pistes. Ski areas typically have one or more chair lifts for moving skiers rapidly to the top of hills, and to interconnect the various pistes. Rope tows can also be used on short slopes (usually beginner hills or bunny slopes). Larger ski areas may use gondolas or aerial trams for transportation across longer distances within the ski area.

A ski resort is a ski area plus amenities to make it a destination resort. This includes a village of accommodations and other amenities adjacent to the ski area. Ski resorts often have other activities to engage in besides skiing and snowboarding, such as snowmobiling, sledding, horse-drawn sleds, dog-sledding, ice-skating, indoor or outdoor swimming and hottubbing, game rooms, and local forms of entertainment, such as clubs, cinema, theatre and cabarets. Ski resorts may be self-contained and entirely devoted to ski tourism (for example Vail ski resort) or they may be near a village or town that had a significant existence before the ski resort was built, such as Jackson Hole, Wyoming or Park City, Utah.

Though skiing is less dangerous than many popular sports (such as bicycling, golf, football, swimming and weightlifting), it is widely perceived as being high risk, in part due to significant accident rates as recently as the 1970s. Nevertheless, ski areas usually have at least a basic first aid facility, and some kind of ski patrol service to ensure that injured skiers are rescued.

The ski patrol is usually responsible for rule enforcement, marking hazards, closing individual runs (if a sufficient level of hazard exists), and removing (dismissing) dangerous participants from the area.

Ski resorts usually have hotels, bars and restaurants that offer après-ski activities, including cocktails, dining and live music. Traditional ski resorts often have health spas with saunas, hot tubs, masseuses, and swimming pools.

A mountain resort is a place to holiday or vacation located in mountains. Common activities include skiing, snowboarding, and ice skating, as well as summer activities such as hiking, mountain biking, golf and tennis.

LIST OF SKI AREAS AND RESORTS

This is a list of ski areas and resorts around the world.

Africa

Lesotho

- Oxbow

Morocco

- Oukaimeden
- Mischliffen

South Africa

- Tiffendell

Asia

List of ski areas and resorts in Asia

This is a list of ski areas and resorts in Asia.

China

- Yabuli Ski Resort, Heilongjiang
- Beidahu, Jilin
- Songhuahu, Jilin
- Nanshan Ski Village, Beijing
- Wanlong Ski Resort, Hebei
- Yulongxueshan, Yunnan
- Xiling Snow-capped Mountain, Chengdu
- Jade Dragon Mountain, Lijiang, Yunnan

Iran

List of ski areas and resorts in Iran

- Dizin
- Shemshak
- Tochal
- Damavand
- Abali
- Darbandsar
- Khor Ski Resort
- Khoshaku

- Sahand Ski Resort
- Kuhrang
- Kakan
- Tarik-darreh
- Alvares
- Sepidan
- Shahmirzad Ski Resort
- Shandiz
- Chelgard
- Jabal Thalgeh
- ShemIran
- Mirdamad

Japan

Hokkaido

- Furano
- Kiroro Snow World
- Niseko
- Rusutsu
- Sahoro
- Tomamu

Tohoku Region

- Appi Kogen
- Hachimantai
- Inawashiro
- Ishiuchi Maruyama
- Kusatsu Shirane
- Myoko Suginohara
- Naeba

- North Shiga Height
- Tazawako
- Tengendai
- Mount Zao

Chubu Region

- Hakuba
- Hakusan Ichirino
- Happo One
- Iizuna Resort
- Nozawa Onsen
- Shiga Kogen
- Sugadaira Kogen
- Sun Alpina
- Togari
- Tsugaike Kogen

Chugoku Region

- Daisen

India

- Gulmarg
- Auli

Kazakhstan

- Shymbulak

Korea

- Alps Resort (Gangwon-do)
- Bears Town (Gangwon-do)
- Daemyung Vivaldi Park (Gangwon-do)

- Gangchon (Gangwon-do)
- Hyundai Sungwoo (Gangwon-do)
- Jisan Forest (Gyeonggi-do)
- Muju (Jeollabuk-do)
- Phoenix Park Resort (Gangwon-do)
- Suanbo Sajo (Chungcheongbuk-do)
- Yangji Pine (Gyeonggi-do)
- Yongpyong (Gangwon-do)

Pakistan

- Malam Jabba

Israel

- Mount Hermon

Lebanon

- The Cedars
- Laqlouq
- Fakra
- Qanat Bakich
- Zaarour
- Faraya Mzaar Kfardebian

Turkey

- Uludag
- Kartalkaya
- Saklikent
- Sarikamis
- Elmadag

- Ilgaz
- Palandoken
- Erciyes

United Arab Emirates

- Ski Dubai

Australasia

List of ski areas and resorts in Australia

Victoria

- Falls Creek
- Lake Mountain
- Mount Baw Baw
- Mount Buffalo
- Mount Buller
- Mount Hotham
- Dinner Plain
- Mount Stirling

New South Wales

- Bullocks Flat
- Charlotte Pass
- Perisher Blue
    - Blue Cow
    - Guthega
    - Perisher Valley
    - Smiggin Holes
- Selwyn snowfields
- Thredbo

Tasmania

- Ben Lomond
- Mount Mawson

North Island

- Whakapapa, Mount Ruapehu
- Tukino, Mount Ruapehu (club skifield)
- Turoa, Mount Ruapehu
- Manganui (club skifield)

South Island

Nelson Lakes

- Rainbow
- Mount Robert

Canterbury

- Fox Peak (club skifield)
- Hanmer Springs Ski Area (club skifield)
- Mount Lyford
- Mount Potts (heliskiing and snowcatting only)
- Mount Hutt
- Mount Dobson
- Ohau
- Porter Heights
- Tasman Glacier (Heliski)
- Temple Basin (club skifield)
- Craigieburn Range
    * Broken River (club skifield)
    * Craigieburn Valley (club skifield)
    * Mount Cheeseman (club skifield)
    * Mount Olympus (club skifield)

Otago

- Coronet Peak
- Invincible Snowfields (helicopter access only)
- The Remarkables
- Round Hill
- Around Wanaka
    * Cardrona Alpine Resort
    * Treble Cone
    * Snow Park
    * Snow Farm (cross-country skiing only)

Andorra

- Ordino-Arcalís
- Pal-Arinsal
- Pas de la Casa-Grau Roig
- Soldeu-El Tarter

Armenia

- Tsakhkadzor ski resort

Austria

Carinthia

- Arnoldstein-Dreiländereck
- Dobratsch (Villacher Alpe--now defunct)
- Gerlitzen
- Heiligenblut
- Innerkrems
- Katschberg
- Koralpe
- Kleinkirchheim

- Nassfeld-Hermagor
- Petzen
- Simonhöhe
- Turracher Höhe

Lower Austria

- Hochkar
- Mitterbach-Gemeindalpe
- Mönichkirchen
- Ötscher (Lackenhof)
- Semmering
- Annaberg

Salzburg

- Gasteinertal (Bad Gastein, Bad Hofgastein, Sportgastein, Dorfgastein, Großarl)
- Hochkönig Area (Mühlbach am Hochkönig, Maria Alm etc.)
- Lungau
- Obertauern
- Saalbach-Hinterglemm
- Salzburger Sportwelt Amadé (including Flachau, Kleinarl, Zauchensee, Altenmarkt, Radstadt, Wagrein etc.)
- Spielbergalm
- Zell am See (including Kaprun, Kitzsteinhorn etc.)
- Dachstein West (including Annaberg im Lammertal, Gosau, Russbach etc.)
- Annaberg im Lammertal

Styria

- Dachstein

- Dachstein-West (Gosau etc.)
- Haus im Ennstal
- Lachtal
- Langenwang
- Schladming
- Stuhleck (Spital am Semmering)
- Tauplitz

Tyrol

- Alpbach
- Arlberg: St. Anton, Lech (actually in Vorarlberg, not Tyrol), Zürs (actually in Vorarlberg, not Tyrol), etc.
- Axamer Lizum
- Innsbruck
- Ischgl-Galtür
- Kitzbühel (including Kirchberg in Tirol, Jochberg, Pass Thurn)
- Lienz
- Ötztal
- Pitztal
- Kaunertal
- Sankt Jakob im Defereggental
- Seefeld
- Stubaital
- Wilder Kaiser Area (Gosau, Scheffau, Ellmau etc.)
- Wildschönau
- Zillertal (including Hintertux)

Upper Austria

- Grünau im Almtal

- Krippenstein
- Postalm
- Loser
- Feuerkogel
- Hinterstoder

Vienna

- Hohe-Wand-Wiese

Vorarlberg

- Schruns-Tschagguns
- Montafon
- Bregenzerwald: Damüls etc.
- Arlberg: Lech, Zürs, Warth, Stuben am Arlberg
- Kleinwalsertal

Bosnia and Herzegovina

- Kupres
- Jahorina
- Bjelasnica
- Igrista
- Blidinje
- Igman
- Vlasic

Bulgaria

- Bansko
- Borovets
- Chepelare
- Pamporovo
- Vitosha

Croatia

- Bjelolasica
- Medvednica
- Platak

Cyprus

- Troodos

Czech Republic

- Špindleruv Mlýn
- Harrachov
- Pec pod Sne□kou

England

- Swinhope (Weardale)
- Yad Moss (Near Alston)
- Raise (Lake District)

Estonia

- Otepää

Finland

- Levi
- Ruka
- Vuokatti
- Ylläs

France

French Alps

- Alpe d'Huez
- Avoriaz
- Bonneval Sur Arc

- Les Carroz
- Chamonix
- Chamrousse
- Chatel
- La Clusaz
- Les Deux Alpes
- Flaine
- Le Grand Bornand
- Les Grand Montets
- Grand-Massif
- Les Houches
- Isola 2000
- Espace Killy (Val d'Isère, Tignes)
- La Plagne
- La Rosière
- Les Arcs
- Les Sybelles (Le courbier, La Toussuire,...)
- Megève
- Montgenèvre
- Morillon
- Notre Dame de Bellecombe
- Orcières Merlette
- Paradiski (Les Arcs, La Plagne, Peisey-Vallandry)
- Risoul
- Samoëns
- Ste. Foy de Tarentaise
- Serre Chevalier
- Sixt Fer a Cheval

- Les Trois Vallées (Courchevel, Méribel with Mottaret, and Val Thorens with Les Menuires and Orelle)
- Les Orres
- Portes du Soleil (Avoriaz, Morzine, Les Gets..., einige in der Schweiz)
- Val Cenis
- Valloire
- Valmorel
- Vars

Pyrenees

- Arette-La Pierre St. Martin
- Bareges/La Mongie
- Cauterets
- Gourette
- Luz Ardiden
- Piau-Engaly
- Somport
- St Lary-Soulan

Vosges

- Gérardmer
- La Bresse
- La Schlucht
- Saint-Maurice-sur-Moselle
- Ventron

Massif Central

- Mont-Dore: 20 ski lifts, 33 ski slopes (42km). 25 km of cross-country skiing
- Super Besse: 22 ski lifts, 25 ski slopes(45 km). 125 km of cross-country skiing

- Super Lioran: 22 ski lifts, 46 ski slopes(60 km). 140 of cross-country skiing

Jura

Georgia

- Bakuriani
- Gudauri

Germany

- Garmisch-Partenkirchen
- Oberstdorf

Greece

- Parnassos
- Kalavrita
- Seli
- 3-5 Pigadia
- Pilio
- Vasilitsa
- Karpenisi
- Voras-Kaimaktsalan
- Lailias
- Pisoderi
- Falakro
- Mainalo
- Gerodovrahos
- Pertouli
- Elatochori
- Metsovo
- Olympus

- Vitsi
- Pagaio

Iceland

- Bláfjöll
- Böggvistaðarfjall
- Dalirnir Tveir
- Hlíðarfjall
- Skarðsdalur
- Skálafell
- Tindastóll

Italy

- Alagna Valsesia
- Alpe Ciamporino by San Domenico di Varzo
- Cervinia
- Cimone
- Dolomiti Superski
- Sulden-Solda
- Courmayeur
- Bormio
- Cortina d'Ampezzo
- Livigno
- Malcesine-Monte Baldo
- Macugnaga
- Passo Di Tonale
- Schnalstal
- Via Lattea (Sestriere, Sauze d'Oulx, Sansicario, Claviere)
- Sella Nevea

Macedonia

- Ko□uf
- Mavrovo
- Popova Šapka
- Kruševo

Norway

- Geilo
- Hafjell in Øyer, near Lillehammer
- Hemsedal
- Kongsberg
- Kvitfjell
- Narvik (alpine skiing)
- Norefjell
- Oppdal
- Sauda alpine and cross-country skiing
- Sirdal
  - * Bjornestad
- Sjusjøen, cross-country skiing
- Stryn, all year glacier skiing
- Tromsø (alpine skiing and cross-country)
- Tryvann in Oslo
- Trysil
- Meråker

Poland

- Zakopane
- Szczyrk
- Ustron

- Wisla
- Karpacz
- Szklarska Poreba
- Czarna Gora
- Bialka Tatrzanska
- Bukowina Tatrzanska
- Krynica Zdroj
- Zawoja

Portugal

- Serra da Estrela (near Loriga)

Romania

- Sinaia
- Predeal
- Poiana Brasov

Russia

- Abzakovo
- Bannoye Lake
- Cheget
- Dombay
- Elbrus
- Kirovsk
- Krasnaya Polyana
- Sheregesh
- Zavyalikha
- Kavgolovo-Toksovo
- Okhta Park
- Zolotaya Dolina

- Krasnoye Ozero
- Snezhny
- Tsey
- Sorochany
- Pukhtolova Gora
- Igora
- Pilnaya
- Panovo
- Yukki Park

Scotland

- Aviemore
- Cairn Gorm
- Glen Coe
- Glenshee Ski Centre
- The Lecht
- Nevis Range
- Highlands of Scotland
- Pentland hills

Serbia

- Kopaonik
- Tara National Park
- Zlatibor
- Stara Planina

Slovakia

- Chopok
- Donovaly
- Jasná

- Starý Smokovec
- Štrbské Pleso
- Tatranská Lomnica
- Vrátna dolina
- □diar

Slovenia

- Cerkno
- Golte near Mozirje
- Kanin near Bovec
- Kobla in Bohinj
- Kope near Slovenj Gradec
- Kranjska Gora
- Krvavec
- Mariborsko Pohorje in Maribor
- Rogla
- Velika planina
- Vogel in Bohinj

Spain

Pyrenees

- Alp 2500 in Baixa Cerdanya (contains La Molina, Spain and Masella)
- Astún
- Baqueira-Beret near Vielha
- Boí-Taüll in Vall de Boí
- Candanchú
- Cerler
- Formigal
- Panticosa-Los Lagos

- Port del Comte
- Rasos de Peguera
- Vallter 2000
- Vall de Núria

Cantabrian Mountains

- Alto Campoo
- Manzaneda
- Valgrande-Pajares
- San Isidro

Sistema Central

- La Covatilla
- La Pinilla
- Navacerrada
- Valdesqui

Iberian Mountains

- Javalambre
- Valdelinares
- Valdezcaray

Sierra Nevada

- Sierra Nevada in Granada

Sweden

- Abisko
- Bjursås
- Björkliden
- Borgafjäll
- Branäs

- Bydalen
- Dundret
- Duved
- Fjätervålen
- Flottsbro in Stockholm
- Funäsdalen
- Hallandsås
- Hemavan
- Hestra
- Hovfjället
- Hundfjället
- Högfjället
- Idre
- Kittelfjäll
- Kläppen
- Lindvallen
- Lofsdalen
- Näsfjället
- Riksgränsen
- Romme near Borlänge
- Storlien
- Storstenshöjden
- Stöten
- Sälen
- Tandådalen
- Tärnaby
- Vemdalen
- Åre

Switzerland

Valais

- Verbier
- Zermatt / Klein Matterhorn
- Crans-Montana
- Saas Fee
- Saas Grund
- Leukerbad
- Anzère
- Nendaz
- Ovronnaz
- Vercorin
- Evolène
- Lötschental
- Grächen
- Visperterminen
- Blatten
- Belalp
- Riederalp
- Bettmeralp
- Fiesch
- Chandolin
- Zinal
- Grimmentz
- Champéry
- Morgins

Bern

- Grindelwald
- Mürren

- Wengen
- Meiringen
- Kandersteg
- Adelboden
- Lenk
- Zweisimmen
- Gstaad

Graubünden

- St. Moritz
- Sils
- Samnaun
- Scuol
- Arosa
- Davos
- Klosters
- Lenzerheide
- Laax
- Flims
- Brigels
- Disentis
- Sedrun
- Obersaxen
- Vals
- Savognin
- Bergün

Central Switzerland

- Engelberg / Titlis
- Melchsee-Frutt

- Andermatt
- Stoos
- Sörenberg

Eastern Switzerland

- Flumserberg
- Pizol / Bad Ragaz
- Braunwald
- Elm
- Wildhaus

Ticino

- Airolo
- Bosco Gurin

Vaud

- Les Diablerets
- Leysin
- Villars
- Château-d'Oex

Ukraine

- Bukovel
- Drahobrat
- Oriavchyk
- Podobovets and Pilipets
- Slavske
- Tisovets

North America

The North American ski season starts as early as October and ends as late as August. The larger ski-able mountains are typically located in the center-west and on the west coast of the continent. Area conditions for many of the areas listed here can be found on the weather network's Ski Report page. An interactive map of ski resort locations can be found at SkiBonk.

Alberta

- Canada Olympic Park (1988 Winter Olympics)
- Canyon Ski Area
- Castle Mountain Resort
- Drumheller Valley Ski Club
- Edmonton Ski Club
- Fairview Ski Hill
- Fortress Mountain
- Hidden Valley Ski Area
- Lake Louise Mountain Resort
- Marmot Basin
- Mount Norquay
- Nakiska (1988 Winter Olympics)
- Nitehawk Ski Area
- Pass Powderkeg
- Rabbit Hill Snow Resort
- Snow Valley Ski Club
- Sunshine Village
- Vista Ridge
- Whispering Pines/Worsley

British Columbia

- Apex Mountain Resort
- Big White Ski Resort

- Crystal Mountain (BC)-Westbank, BC
- Cypress Mountain (2010 Winter Olympics)
- Fairmont Hot Springs Resort
- Fernie Alpine Resort
- Grouse Mountain
- Harper Mountain
- Hemlock Valley
- Kicking Horse Resort
- Kimberley Alpine Resort
- Manning Park (Gibson Pass)
- Mount Baldy Ski Area
- Mount Cain Alpine Park
- Mount Seymour
- Mount Washington Alpine Resort
- Panorama Mountain Village
- Phoenix Mountain Ski Resort
- Powder King Mountain Resort
- Powder Springs Ski Area
- Red Resort
- Revelstoke Mountain Resort
- Salmo Ski Area
- Shames Mountain
- Silver Star Mountain Resort
- Ski Smithers
- Summit Lakes
- Sun Peaks Resort
- Troll Ski Resort
- Whistler-Blackcomb Resort (2010 Winter Olympics)

- Whitewater Ski Resort
- Pantheon Helisports

Manitoba

- Asessippi Ski Area
- Falcon Ridge Ski Area
- Holiday Mountain
- Mystery Mountain Winter Resort
- Stony Mountain Ski Area

New Brunswick

- Crabbe Mountain
- Mount Farlagne
- Poley Mountain
- Sugarloaf

Newfoundland

- Marble Mountain
- Smokey Mountain

Nova Scotia

- Cape Smokey
- Ski Ben Eoin
- Ski Martock
- Ski Wentworth

Ontario

- Batawa Ski Hill
- Beaver Valley Ski Club
- Blue Mountain
- Boler Mountain

- Calabogie Peaks
- Caledon Ski Club
- Centennial Park
- Chicopee (ski area)
- Cobble Hills Ski Club
- Dagmar (Ski area)
- Devil's Elbow
- Devil's Glen Country Club
- Georgian Peaks Club
- Glen Eden
- Gravenhurst Nordic Trails
- Hardwood Hills
- Hidden Valley Highlands
- Highlands Nordic
- Hockley Valley
- Horseshoe Valley
- Kamiskotia Snow Resort
- Lakeridge Ski Resort
- Laurentian Ski Hill
- Loch Lomond Ski Area
- London Ski Club at Boler
- Mansfield Outdoor Center
- Mansfield Ski Club
- Mount Chinguacousy
- Mount Pakenham
- Mount St. Louis Moonstone
- Mountain View Ski Area
- North York Ski Center

- Oshawa Ski Club
- Osler Bluff Ski Club
- Pine Ridge Ski Club
- Sir Sam's Ski Area
- Skyloft Ski Country Club
- Superior Slopes
- Searchmont Resort
- Snow Valley (ski area)
- Talisman (ski area)
- Trestle Ridge Ski Slopes
- Uplands Ski Area

Québec

- Belle Neige
- Bellevue (ski area)
- Bromont
- Club Tobo-Ski
- Camp Fortune
- Edelweiss Valley
- Grey Rocks
- La Tuque
- Le Massif
- Le Relais
- La Valinouet
- Massif du Sud
- Mont Adstock
- Mont Alta
- Mont Blanc
- Mont Cascades

- Mont Castor
- Mont Chalco
- Mont Edouard
- Mont Fortin
- Mont Gabriel
- Mont Gleason
- Mont Grand Fonds
- Mont Habitant
- Mont Kanasula
- Mont Lac Vert
- Mont Olympia
- Mont Orford
- Mont Orignal
- Mont Rigaud
- Mont Saint-Bruno
- Mont Saint-Mathieu
- Mont Saint-Sauveur
- Mont Shefford
- Mont Sutton
- Mont Villa Saguenay
- Mont-Garceau
- Mont-Sainte-Anne, Quebec
- Mont Ste-Marie
- Mont-Video
- Montjoye
- Morin Heights
- Owl's Head
- Parc du Mont-Comi

- Pin Rouge
- Ski Chanteder
- Ski La Reserve
- Ski Montcalm
- Ski Sutton Inc.
- Station de neige St-Pacome
- Station de Ski Gallix
- Stoneham
- Tremblant
- Val Mauricie
- Val Negigette Inc
- Val Saint Come
- Val-d'Irene
- Vallee Bleue
- Vallee du Parc
- Vorlage

Saskatchewan

- Table Mountain Ski Resort

Yukon Territory

- Mt Sima
- Watson Lake

LUXURY RESORT

A luxury resort, sometimes referred to as an exclusive resort, is a very expensive vacation facility which is fully staffed and has been rated with five stars. Luxury resorts often boast many visitor activities and attractions such as golf, watersports, spa and beauty facilities, skiing, natural ecology and tranquillity. Because of the extent of amenities offered, a luxury resort is also considered a destination resort.

A luxury resort is an elite luxury property which exhibits an exceptionally high degree of customer service and hospitality. A flawless execution of guest services will be the resort staff's and management's main concern. A luxury resort will commonly also feature a superb architectural interior and exterior design as well as an interesting physical location.

The interior design will normally be elegant with stylish bedroom decor, exceptional dining facilities, and manicured landscaping and meticulous grounds. Luxury resorts will often also be in based in exceptionally desirable and strategic worldwide locations, from beautiful tropical islands, to snow caked mountains, to scenic lakes and rivers, to exhilarating cities. The locations will often be famous for featured activities from skiing to golf, water spots, diving, fishing, sailing and nature walks to glamorous shopping and nightlife entertainment.

A luxury resort may vary greatly in character, style and theme from resort to resort. A luxury resort will, however, normally be characterized by a high level of luxury, sophistication and, of course, price. Accommodations are first class, whether they follow a classic and traditional nature or a more minimalist and modern styling. An unmatched level of comfort will be available at a luxury resort, as well as many personalized services and amenities.

Bolivia

- Chacaltaya
- Mururata

Argentina

- Caviahue
- Cerro Bayo
- Cerro Catedral (Bariloche)
- Cerro Castor

- Chapelco
- Glacier El Martial
- La Hoya
- Las Leñas
- Los Penitentes
- Perito Moreno
- Valdelen
- Vallecitos
- Valle Manantiales
- Wolfgang Wallner

Chile

- Portillo
- Chapa Verde
- El Colorado-Farellones
- Lagunillas
- La Parva
- Valle Nevado
- Antillanca
- Antuco
- Cerro Mirador
- La Burbuja
- Llaima
- Lonquimay
- Termas De Chillán
- Pucón-Volcán Villarrica
- Valle El Arpa
- Los Arenales
- Cerro El Fraile

- Corralco
- Las Araucarias
- Huilo-Huilo
- Lagunillas
- Volcán Osorno-Puerto Varas

Peru

- Callejón de Huaylas
- Pasto-Ruri/Huascarán

Venezuela

- Mérida

County Clare

Lahinch is a bustling seaside resort, and is very popular for holidaymakers because of its long beach, golf links, promenade, and Seaworld (a leisure complex). Lahinch is extremely popular with surfers.

Ballyvaughan is a village and small port on the southern shores of Galway Bay and is a convenient centre for exploring the fascinating and scenic surrounding countryside.

CANADA'S GRAND RAILWAY HOTELS

Canada's railway hotels are a series of grand hotels across the country, each a local and national landmark, and most of which are icons of Canadian history and architecture. Each hotel was originally built by the Canadian railway companies, or the railways acted as a catalyst for the hotel's construction, and the hotels were intended to serve the passengers of the country's then expanding rail network.

Architecture

Many of the railway hotels were built in the "château style" (also termed the "neo-château" or "châteauesque" style), which as a result became known as a distinctly Canadian form of architecture.

The use of towers and turrets, and other Scottish baronial and French château architectural elements, became a signature style of Canada's majestic hotels, and was even borrowed by the designers of important public buildings (such as the Confederation and Justice buildings in Ottawa).

In later years, the railway companies departed from the château style for some of their properties, notably with the construction of Winnipeg's Royal Alexandra in 1906, the Palliser Hotel in Calgary, built in 1914, and the elaborate second Hotel Vancouver, which was done in grand Italianate style quite unlike any of the other Canadian railway hotels.

History

Canada's first grand railway hotel, the Windsor Hotel in Montreal, opened in 1878. Although it was not owned by a railway company, it was built to serve railway visitors from nearby Windsor Station.

Given its location next to Montreal's main train station, the Windsor served for years as the permanent residence of executives of both the Canadian Pacific Railway and Grand Trunk Railway.

The direct involvement of the railways in the construction and operation of large hotels originated with Canadian Pacific Railway's opening of the Hotel Vancouver on May 16, 1888. This was the first of three railway owned hotels by that name in Vancouver.

Two weeks later, the Banff Springs Hotel was officially opened by the Canadian Pacific Railway on June 1, 1888. CPR president William Cornelius Van Horne had personally chosen the site in the Rocky Mountains for the new hotel, and he envisioned a string of grand hotels across Canada that would draw visitors from abroad to his railway. Van Horne famously remarked: "If we can't export the scenery, we'll import the tourists." (Chisholm, 2001:12) The original Banff Springs Hotel, of wooden construction, was accidentally destroyed by fire in 1926 and replaced by the present structure.

Canadian Pacific Hotels next built the Château Frontenac in Quebec City, which quickly came to be the symbol of the city and was designed to rival any hotel in Europe. Its elevated location overlooking the city also made it a readily identifiable landmark as viewed from passing trains as well as ships plying the waters of the Saint Lawrence River en route to Montreal. Place Viger followed in Montreal, followed by The Empress in Victoria, British Columbia and the Château Lake Louise in Alberta.

The CPR's main competitor, the Grand Trunk Railway, was not prepared to leave the field solely to its rival, and it was similarly determined to build a chain of luxury hotels across the country, even borrowing the château style from the CPR. The GTR built the Château Laurier in Ottawa in 1912, with the Fort Garry Hotel in Winnipeg and the Hotel Macdonald in Edmonton following in 1913 and 1915 respectively.

The GTR was amalgamated into the Canadian National Railway in 1920. During the decades that followed, the CPR and the CNR continued to expand their competing hotel chains across the country. The Queen Elizabeth Hotel in Montreal, built in 1958 over that city's Gare Centrale (Central Station), was perhaps the last true railway hotel built in Canada, although both chains continued to open new establishments in subsequent years (albeit none of them had any connection to the railways, except through their ownership).

In 1988, Canadian Pacific acquired the CNR hotels, and for the first time, many of Canada's railway hotels were operated by the same chain. In 1999, Canadian Pacific Hotels became Fairmont Hotels and Resorts, borrowing a name of a company it had recently acquired. Although Fairmont continues to operate many of Canada's landmark hotels, some of the historic railway hotels are owned and managed by other hotel chains.

National Icons

Despite their age, Canada's railway hotels remain national icons. It is hard to imagine Victoria without the Empress, the Rockies without the Banff Springs or the Chateau Lake Louise, Toronto without the Royal York, Ottawa without the Château Laurier or Quebec City without the Chateau Frontenac.

3

The Sanatorium

INTRODUCTION

A sanatorium (also sanitorium, sanitarium) is a medical facility for long-term illness, typically tuberculosis. A distinction was sometimes made between a "sanitarium" (a kind of health resort, as in the Battle Creek Sanitarium) and "sanatorium" (a hospital).

According to the Saskatchewan Lung Association, when the National Anti-Tuberculosis Association was founded in 1904, it was felt that a distinction should be made between the health resorts with which people were familiar and the new tuberculosis treatment hospitals: "So they decided to use a new word which instead of being derived from the Latin noun sanitas, meaning health, would emphasize the need for scientific healing or treatment. Accordingly, they took the Latin verb root sano, meaning to heal, and adopted the new word sanatorium".

The rationale for sanitoriums was that before antibiotic treatments existed, a regime of rest and good nutrition offered the best chance that the sufferer's immune system would 'wall off' pockets of pulmonary tuberculosis infection.

In the early twentieth century, tuberculosis sanatoriums (or sanatoria) were common in the United States. The first tuberculosis sanatorium for blacks was Burkeville, Virginia's Piedmont Sanatorium. Waverly Hills Sanatorium, a

Louisville, Kentucky tuberculosis sanatorium, was founded in 1911. It has become a mecca for curiosity-seekers who believe it is haunted. A.G. Holley Hospital in Lantana, Florida is the last remaining freestanding tuberculosis sanatorium in the United States.

Switzerland had many sanatoriums, as it was believed that clean mountain air was the best treatment for lung diseases. The ill of Europe were sent to recover there. The Heliantia Sanatorium in Valadares, Portugal was used for the treatment of bone tuberculosis between the 1930s and 1960s.

After 1943, when Albert Schatz, a graduate student at Rutgers University, discovered Streptomycin, the first true cure for tuberculosis, sanatoriums began to close. Around the 1950's, tuberculosis was no longer a major public health threat and so most of the sanatoriums had reached the end of their lives. Most sanatoriums were demolished years ago.

Some, however, have assumed updated medical roles. The Tambaram Sanatorium in south India is now a hospital of excellence for AIDS patients. The state hospital in Sanatorium, Mississippi is now a regional mental retardation center.

FORMER SOVIET UNION

In the former Soviet Union the term has a slightly different meaning. It is mostly a combination of a resort/ recreational facility and a medical facility intended to provide short-term complex rest and medical services.

IN LITERATURE

The Magic Mountain (Der Zauberberg), a novel by the German author Thomas Mann (1875-1955), is set in a sanatorium. Mann was familiar with this type of setting from 1912 when his wife was hospitalized with lung disease for several months in Dr Friedrich Jessen's Waldsanatorium in Davos, Switzerland. Der Zauberberg, one of the most influential of all 20th-century novels, is a lengthy work and was first published in two volumes by S. Fischer Verlag in 1924.

LOSHENG SANATORIUM

Losheng Sanatorium (Traditional Chinese: Pinyin: lèsheng liáoyangyuàn) is a hospital for lepers, which is located in Hsinchuang City, Taipei County, Taiwan. Losheng means "happy life". It was constructed in the 1930s during the Japanese colonial period. At present there has been heated debates and protests about the plans to replace Losheng Sanatorium with a MRT (Mass Rapid Transport) depot.

History

Losheng Sanatorium, originally named Rakusei Sanatorium for Lepers of Governor-General of Taiwan (Taiwan Sotokufu Raibyo Rakuseiin?), was built in 1929 during the Japanese colonial period and served as an isolation hospital for leprosy patients at that time. The Japanese government forced leprosy patients to live in this hospital. The first 5 buildings could house more than 100 patients.

During the 1930s, Losheng Sanatorium was the first leprosy hospital and the only public sanatorium for leprosy patients in Taiwan. It was designed for quarantine and treatment of lepers. With the force of sanitary police and medical officers, investigation, quarantine, and imprisonment of lepers were conducted thoroughly in the period from 1934 till the end of colonial governance of Japan. As a result, Losheng Sanatorium became the institution of compulsory quarantine as well as life-long imprisonment for thousands of leprosy patients. The successive KMT regime inherited the policy in its early years.

After the discovery of new Leprosy treatment, patients were later allowed to leave Losheng Sanatorium since 1954. However, many of them who had undergone chronic isolation and faced discrimination had little choice but to stay and have grown used to the settings.

In 1994, the Department of Taipei Rapid Transit System (DORTS) planned to build a depot in the site where Losheng Sanatorium is. Although the government built a new hospital building nearby for settling the patients, the demolish of original compound still brought a series of debates and later preservation movement. According to the survey conducted in March 2006, there are still 165 Losheng residents living in the new hospital building and 52 living in the old compound or other places.

Debates and Preservation Movement

In 1994, Taipei Rapid Transit System planned to build a depot on the site where now the Sanatorium is. Chen Ching-Chuan, the ex-director of Losheng was opposed to this decision, and did three surveys among the patients to see what they thought and needed, shortly before he got demoted and reprimanded. Ever since then, the patients had no access to the MRT construction plans and its related discussions.

Fight for Preservation

In 2001, due to the construction of Hsinchuang Line, the government planned to transform Losheng to a community hospital, thus put an end to its dedicated hospitalization and care for leprosy patients. Many students, urban planners and NGO tried to protect this sanatorium ever since then.

In 2002, the new housing projects, Huei Long Hospital was initiated, but instead of 'houses' which were earlier promised to the patients, the new director gave them two tall buildings with modern hospital facilities. It became clear that the new administration team intended to run a hospital business and make money. The skyscraper-ish hospital buildings were designed mainly for housing short-term patients; therefore it has inadequate space for residents to move around freely. Moreover, the hospital management team forbids the patients from bringing with them personal belongings, from cooking, and from coming over to the front building, which policy is nothing less than discriminative.

Long before the depot construction was initiated, Loshen's ex-director and history professionals have demanded a large-scale inspection of Losheng's position as a historical site. The scholars appealed to the MRT Department that they should spare the Losheng Sanatorium, while they unanimously agreed the entire site should be preserved. However, the officials unilaterally terminated the process of inspection, and decided the Sanatorium should be torn down entirely.

It was not until 2004, when Prof. John K.C. Liu came up with a symbiosis plan, and when the Council for Cultural Affairs has deemed the Sanatorium a historical spot, that the MRT Department was pressured to rethink the possibilities of preservation.

Reasons for Preservation

People who claimed that the Losheng Sanatorium should be preserved have raised the following issues:

The MRT depot was originally planned to be built Yingpan near Fu Jen Catholic University (FJU,), and FJU station should be terminal station. That's why the number of that station is O1, meaning "first station of Orange Line".

But the plan was altered by local politicians. It has been asserted that this is wrong for the following reasons:

1. Waste of money: 3/5 of the depot site needs to be built on flatland; therefore $90 million (USD) will be spent on flatting and improving the soil.
2. Disaster for the environment: What comes after flatting the mountains is a ten-story-tall retaining wall, which destroys the natural environment.
3. Safety concern: the future depot will be situated upon earth faults.

4. Ravaged historical site: the Losheng Sanatorium is an important cultural asset for people in East Asia. The depot construction will turn all this treasure into dust.
5. Ordeal for patients: the patients are forced to leave the place they spent their lives, suffering mentally and physically from the displacement.
6. Autocratic decision-making: the MRT Department never inquired the needs of Losheng patients--the 'residents' of the site-which is a violation of fundamental human rights.

Furthermore, they argued that the Losheng Sanatorium should be an accredited World Heritagesite for it has witnessed the inhumane treatment (such as discrimination and compulsory quarantine) inflicted on the lepers, who had undergone 70 years of governmental oppression.

Doubts for the Plan

In the press release issued by the Council for Cultural Affairs (CCA) in Jan. 23, 2007, it was mentioned: "according to recent news, some local representatives and organizations in Taipei City and Taipei County claimed that the 90% Losheng preservation plan proposed by CCA will severely delay the MRT construction. Hereby CCA reiterates that the 90% preservation plan, evaluated by Hsin-Lu cooperation, will lengthen the construction period for about four months, and appends a three billion budget to it.

It is not true to say the MRT construction will be delayed for two to three years." This press release concludes that it is untrue for the media and Department of Taipei Rapid Transit System (DORTS, Taipei) to say that the 90% preservation plan will delay the construction of MRT for two to three years and result in a two to three hundred billion NTD (approx. 760 million USD) increase in budget.

Timeline

March 11, 2007

The activists held a sit-in protest in front of Premier Su Tseng-chang's house, and demanded to negotiate with the Premier himself. The protestors, consisting of students and remaining Losheng patients, were later forced by the police into buses and immediately transported to suburban mountainous areas around Taipei City, and were ordered not to return to the scene that day.

March 16, 2007

There were scuffles as the authorities attempted to post the official notice issued by the Taipei County government to request the management of sanatorium to tear down the structure by April 16, 2007. Four students were arrested, and the protest organizers condemned police for the unnecessary violence against protesters.

April 15, 2007

A protest march of thousands of people from all over the country took place in Taipei on the day which had been announced for the eviction of the remaining 45 residents of the Sanatorium. Hsu Po-jen of the Youth Alliance for Losheng was reported as saying that more than 100 civic groups took part.

May 30, 2007

The Public Construction Commission of Executive Yuan ruled that 39 buildings of Losheng Sanatorium should be preserved, 10 to be reconstructed or reconstituted in selected locations, and 6 to be demolished. The project budget would increase NTD 670 million.

NIGHTCLUB

A nightclub (or "night club" or "club") is a drinking, dancing, and entertainment venue which does its primary business after dark. A nightclub is usually distinguished from bars, pubs or taverns, by the inclusion of a dance floor and a DJ booth, where a DJ plays recorded dance and pop music. Some nightclubs have other forms of entertainment, such as comedians, "go-go" dancers, a floor show or strippers (see strip club).

The music in nightclubs is either live bands or, more commonly a mix of songs played by a DJ through a powerful PA system. Most clubs or club nights cater to certain music genres, such as house music, techno, drum'n'bass, hip-hop, or salsa. In the US, the largest nightclubs are found in New York, Miami, Chicago, Las Vegas, San Francisco, Atlanta, and Los Angeles. Elsewhere in the world, nightclubs congregate in major and capital cities, although often even very small towns and cities feature at least one nightclub, often the sole focus for weekend late night activities.

Nightclubs often feature lighting and other effects, to enhance the dancing experiences. Lighting and effects include flashing colored lights, moving light beams, laser light shows, strobe lights, a mirror-covered disco balls, or foam, and smoke machines.

Nightclub hours vary widely; depending on the liquor regulations in a region, in the U.S nightclubs may stay open until 1 AM or even 4 AM. In some cities, illegal "after hours" clubs stay open and serve alcohol after the legal closing time. However, in many other countries such as the United Kingdom, Japan and Australia, nightclubs stay open legally all night and into early daylight hours.

In most other languages, nightclubs are referred to as "discos" or "discothèques" (French: discothèque; Italian and Spanish: discoteca; German: Disko or Diskothek). In Japanese, disuko refers to an older, smaller, less fashionable venue; while ?, kurabu refers to a more recent, larger, more popular venue. The term night is used to refer to an evening focusing on a specific genre, such as "retro music night" or a "singles night."

Types of Clubs

Variant types of nightclubs include non-smoking and alcohol-free nightclubs, or comedy clubs. Restaurants or supper clubs may provide music and entertainment similar to that provided by a nightclub. However, the food is the main attraction at these establishments, whereas entertainment is the main attraction at a nightclub. Another type of club is a concert club, which specializes in hosting performances of live music. In contrast to regular night clubs, concert clubs are usually only open when a performance is scheduled. Another type of nightclub is the under 18's kind, this is usually one night a week/month where the nightclub opens business for those usually over 14 and under 18. On these nights alcohol isn't served and chewing gum is sometimes forbidden too. These under 18's nights are especially popular for schoolkids in the UK.

Nightclubs are usually built in former warehouses and cinemas, underground buildings, and custom-built buildings, with thick, insulated walls and few or no windows, so that the neighboring buildings will not be disturbed by the powerful beat of the dance music and the flashing strobe lights. As well, this style of construction keeps light and noise from the street from entering the club. This allows the nightclub to turn the dance floor into an alternate, illusory realm of timelessness. Even if an all-night rave at a nightclub lasts until 6 AM, when it is light outside, to the clubgoers, it is still dark inside the club, and the partying and dancing continue.

In most cases entering a night club requires a flat fee called a cover charge. Early arrivers and women often have cover waived, though (in the United Kingdom at least), this latter option is illegal under the Sex Discrimination Act 1975. Friends of the doorman or the club owner may gain free entrance. Sometimes, especially at larger clubs, one only gets a pay card at the entrance, on which all money spent in the discotheque (often including the entrance fee) is marked. Sometimes entrance fee and wardrobe costs are paid by cash and only the drinks in the club are paid using a pay card.

History

During US Prohibition, nightclubs went underground as illegal speakeasies. With the repeal of Prohibition in February 1933 nightclubs were revived, such as New York's Stork Club, El Morocco and the Copacabana. In Harlem, the Cotton Club was king. Before 1953 and even some years thereafter, most bars and nightclubs used a jukebox or mostly live bands. In Paris, at a club named Whisky à Gogo, Régine laid down a dance-floor, suspended coloured lights and replaced the juke-box with two turntables which she operated herself so there would be no breaks between the music. The Whisky à Gogo set into place the standard elements of the modern discotheque-style nightclub.

In the early 1960s, Mark Birley opened a members-only discotheque nightclub, Annabel's, in Berkeley Square, London. However, the first rock and roll generation preferred rough and tumble bars and taverns to elegant nightclubs, and the nightclub did attain mainstream popularity until the 1970s disco era. By the late 1970s many major US cities had thriving disco club scenes which were centered around discotheques, nightclubs, and private loft parties where DJs would play disco hits through powerful PA systems for the dancers. The DJs played "... a smooth mix of long single records to keep people "dancing all night long" " Some of the most prestigious clubs had elaborate lighting systems that throbbed to the beat of the music.

Some cities had disco dance instructors or dance schools which taught people how to do popular disco dances such as "touch dancing", the "hustle" and the "cha cha." There were also disco fashions that discotheque-goers wore for nights out at their local disco, such as sheer, flowing Halston dresses for women and shiny polyester Qiana shirts for men. Disco clubs and "...hedonistic loft parties" had a club culture which had many African American, gay" and hispanic people.

In addition to the dance and fashion aspects of the disco club scene, there was also a thriving drug subculture, particularly for drugs that would enhance the experience of dancing to the loud music and the flashing lights, such as cocaine (nicknamed "blow"), amyl nitrite "poppers", and the "...other quintessential 1970s club drug Quaalude, which suspended motor coordination and turned one's arms and legs to Jell-O."

The "[m]assive quantities of drugs ingested in discotheques by newly liberated gay men produced the next cultural phenomenon of the disco era: rampant promiscuity and public sex. While the dance floor was the central arena of seduction, actual sex usually took place in the nether regions of the disco: bathroom stalls, exit stairwells, and so on. In other cases the disco became a kind of "main course" in a hedonist's menu for a night out."

Famous 1970s discotheques included "...cocaine-filled celeb hangouts such as Manhattan's Studio 54 ", which was operated by Steve Rubell and Ian Schrager. Studio 54 was notorious for the hedonism that went on within; the balconies were known for sexual encounters, and drug use was rampant. Its dance floor was decorated with an image of the "Man in the Moon" that included an animated cocaine spoon. Other famous discotheques included the Loft, the Paradise Garage, and Aux Puces, one of the first gay disco bars.

By the early 1980s, the term "disco" had largely fallen out of favor in North America). Today in Europe, nightclubs play the disco-influenced dance music called house music, techno, and other dance music styles such as electro or trance. Most nightclubs in the U.S. major cities such as New York, Los Angeles, Las Vegas, Chicago, Dallas, Atlanta, Miami, Detroit, and San Francisco play hip-hop, house and trance music. These clubs are generally the largest and most frequented of all of the different types of clubs.

THE HOTEL BARS

INTRODUCTION

A bar (also called a pub or tavern) is a business that serves drinks, especially alcoholic beverages such as beer, liquor, and mixed drinks, for consumption on the premises. Bars provide stools or chairs for the patrons along tables or raised counters. Some bars have entertainment on a stage, such as a live band, comedians, go-go dancers, a floor show or strippers (see strip club). Bars that are part of hotels are sometimes called long bars or hotel lounges.

The term "bar" is derived from the specialized counter on which drinks are served and is a synecdoche applied to the whole of the drinking establishment. The "back bar" or "gantry" is a set of shelves of glasses and bottles behind that counter. In some bars, the gantry is elaborately decorated with woodwork, etched glass, mirrors, and lights. When food is served elsewhere in the establishment, it may also be ordered and eaten at the bar.

KINDS OF BARS

There are many types of bars, which can be categorized according to the types of entertainment provided at the bar and by their clientèle.

Bars categorized by the type of entertainment or activities offered at the bar include: Topless bars, where topless female employees serve drinks or dance; sports bars, where sports fans watch games on large-screen televisions; salsa bars, where patrons dance to latin salsa music; and dance bars, which have a modest-siced dance floor where patrons dance to recorded music. However, if a dance bar has a large dance floor and hires well-known professional DJs, it is usually considered to be nightclub or discothèque.

Bars categorized by the clientele who come to the bar include: biker bars, which are bars frequented by motorcycle enthusiasts, bikerbars, and in some regions, motorcycle gang members; gay bars, where gay men or women dance and socialize; cop bars, where off-duty law enforcement agents gather; and singles bars where (mostly) unmarried people of both genders can socialize and meet.

A bar owners and managers typically chose establishment names, decor, drink menus, lighting and other elements they can control so as to attract a certain clientele. However, bar operators have only limited influence over who patronizes their establishments and a bar envisioned for one demographic can become popular with another. For example, a gay bar with a dance floor might attract an increasingly-straight clientele over time and vice versa. As well, a blues club may become a de facto "biker bar" if its main clients are biker gang members.

There are also retro bars and lounge bars.

BARS AROUND THE WORLD

United States

In the United States of America, legal distinctions often exist between restaurants, bars, and even types of bars. These distinctions vary from state to state, and even among municipalities. Beer bars (sometimes called taverns or pubs) may be legally restricted to only selling beer or possibly wine, cider and other low-proof beverages. Liquor bars sell everything from beer to hard liquor.

Bars are sometimes exempt from smoking bans that restaurants are subject to, even if those restaurants have liquor licenses. The distinction between a restaurant that serves liquor and a bar is usually made by the percentage of revenue earned from selling liquor, although increasingly, smoking bans include bars too.

In most places, bars are prohibited from selling alcoholic beverages to go and this makes them clearly different from liquor stores. Some brewpubs and wineries can serve alcohol to go, but under the rules applied to a liquor store. In some areas, such as New Orleans and parts of Las Vegas, open containers of alcohol may be prepared to go. This kind of restriction is usually dependent on open container law. In Pennsylvania and Ohio, bars may sell six packs of beer "to-go" in original (sealed) containers by obtaining a take-out license.

Historically, the western United States featured saloons. Many saloons survive in the western United States, though their services and features have changed with the times. Newer establishments have been built in the saloon style to duplicate the feeling of the older establishments.

Many Irish or British-themed "pubs" exist throughout United States and Canada and in some continental European countries. These bars serve British ales, stouts, and lagers and liquors such as single-malt whiskey in establishments that recreate the appearance of an old British pub. Typically, these pub-style bars furnish the bar with wood panelling and private booths, and decorate the walls with advertisements for Guinness Stout and other well-known UK brands.

Canada

As a former British dominion, Canada absorbed many of the bar traditions common in the UK, such as the drinking of dark ales and stouts, and the establishment of British-style pubs. Canada adopted the UK-style tavern, which was the most popular type of bar throughout the 1960s and 1970s, especially for working class people. Canadian taverns, which can still be found in remote regions of Northern Canada, have long tables with benches lining the sides. Patrons in the smoky taverns order beer in large quart bottles and drink inexpensive "bar brand" Canadian rye whisky. Originally, taverns had separate entrances for men and women, in order to protect decorum.

As Canada borders the United States, it has also adopted many U.S. bar traditions, such as the "biker bar", the "country bar", and the blues bar. The U.S.-style sports bar has become very popular in Canada. Canadian sports bars are usually decorated with merchandise and paraphenalia featuring the local hockey team, and patrons watch the games on large-screen televisions.

Legal restrictions on bars are set by the Canadian provinces and territories, which has led to a great deal of variety. While some provinces have been very restrictive with their bar regulation, setting strict closing times and banning the removal of alcohol from the premises, other provinces have been more liberal. In Alberta, for example, patrons can order beer for "take-out" at the end of the night, a practice which is illegal in provinces such as Ontario. In some provinces, such as Quebec, patrons can drink until 3 a.m.

United Kingdom & Ireland

In the UK and Ireland, bars are either areas that serve alcoholic drinks within establishments such as hotels, restaurants, universities, or are a particular type of establishment which serves alcoholic drinks such as wine bars, "style bars", private membership only bars. However the main type of establishment selling alcohol for consumption on the premises is the public house or pub. Some bars are similar to nightclubs in that they feature loud music, subdued lighting, or operate a dress code and admissions policy, with inner city bars generally having bouncers at the entrance.

Australia

In Australia, traditionally the 'public bar' was where only men drank, while the 'lounge bar' or 'saloon bar' was where women or men could drink (i.e. mixed drinking). This distinction is not seen now as anti-discrimination legislation and women's rights activism has broken down the concept of a public drinking area accessible to only one sex. Where two bars still exist in the one establishment, one (that derived from the 'public bar') will be more downmarket while the other (deriving from the 'lounge bar') will be more upmarket.

Over time, with the introduction of gaming machines into hotels, many 'lounge bars' have or are being converted into gaming rooms. In the major Australian cities there is an immense and diverse bar scene with a range of ambiences, modes and styles catering for every echelon of cosmopolitan society. Melbourne maintains a strong hold of the up and coming drinking scene.

Italy

In Italy, a 'bar' is a place more similar to a Café, where people go during the morning or the afternoon, usually to take a coffee, a cappuccino, a hot chocolate and eat some kind of snack like pastries and sandwiches (panini or tramezzini). However, any kind of alcoholic beverages are served. Opening hours vary: some establishments are open since very early in the morning and close relatively early in the evening; others, especially if next to a theater or a cinema, may be open until late at night. In larger cities like Milan, Rome, Turin or Genoa, many larger bars are also restaurants and disco clubs. Many Italian bars have introduced a 'so called' "aperitivo" time in the evening: everyone who purchases an alcoholic drink then has free access to an usually abundant buffet of cold dishes like pasta salads, vegetables and various types of appetizers.

Spain

Bars in Spain are very common and form an important part in Spanish culture. Spanish bars are known for freely serving snacks called tapas or pintxos. Spain has more bars per capita than any other country in the world, with close to 6 bars per thousand inhabitants--three times more than the UK and four times more than Germany..

Elsewhere

In most cities of the world there is at least one Irish pub. Most major cities such as Brussels and New York City have more than twenty. Bars range from down-and-dirty "dives" which are little more than a dark room with a counter and some bottles of liquor, to elegant places of entertainment for the elite.

Many bars set a happy hour to encourage off-peak patronage. Contrastingly, bars that fill to capacity typically implement a cover charge, often similar in price to one or two cocktails, during their peak hours. Such bars often feature entertainment, which may be a live band, a popular D.J., or a variety (female impersonation) show.

BAR-RELATED TRIVIA

- The longest bar in the world is 684 feet or about 208.5 meters long and is located at the New Bulldog in Rock Island, Illinois.
- A bar is now located in the New York City building that once housed the National Temperance Society.
- The United States Marine Corps' first recruiting station was in a bar.
- Actors Tom Arnold, Sandra Bullock, Chevy Chase, Bill Cosby, and Bruce Willis, and musicians Dave Matthews, Kris Kristofferson, and Rob Dougan are all former bartenders.

4

THE PUBLIC HOUSE

INTRODUCTION

A public house, usually known as a pub, is an establishment which serves alcoholic drinks especially beer for consumption on the premises, usually in a cozy setting. Pubs are commonly found in English-speaking countries, particularly in the United Kingdom, Ireland, Canada, Australia and New Zealand.

In North America, drinking establishments with a British or Irish name or theme are called pubs as well; the appellation "pub" itself is often a component of this theme. Although the terms may have different connotations, there is no definitive difference between pubs, bars, taverns and lounges where alcohol is served commercially.

Traditionally, a pub which offers lodging may be called an inn or (more recently) hotel in the UK. Today many pubs, in the UK and Australia in particular, with the word "inn" or "hotel" in their name no longer offer accommodation, or in some cases have never done so.

Some pubs often bear the name of "hotel" because they are in countries where stringent anti-drinking laws were once necessary. Until 1976 in Scotland only hotels could serve alcohol on Sundays; in Australia, this restriction operated all through the week.

OVERVIEW OF BRITISH PUBS

There are approximately 60,000 public houses in the United Kingdom, with one in almost every village. In many places, especially in villages, a pub can be the focal point of the community, playing a similar role to the local church in this respect.

Public houses are culturally and socially different from places such as cafés, bars, bierkellers and brewpubs.

Pubs are social places based on the sale and consumption of alcoholic beverages, and most public houses offer a range of beers, wines, spirits, alcopops and soft drinks. Many pubs are controlled by breweries, so beer is often better value than wines and spirits, whilst soft drinks can be almost as expensive. Beer served in a pub may be cask ale or keg beer.

The beer lends most pubs a pleasant, memorable aroma. All pubs also have a range of non-alcoholic beverages available. Traditionally the windows of town pubs are of smoked or frosted glass so that the clientele is obscured from the street. In the last twenty years in the UK and other countries there has been a move away from frosted glass towards clear glass, a trend which fits in with brighter interior decors.

The owner, tenant or manager (licensee) of a public house is known as the publican or landlord. Each pub generally has a crowd of regulars, people who drink there regularly. The pub that people visit most often is called their local. In many cases, this will be the pub nearest to their home, but some people choose their local for other reasons: proximity to work, a traditional venue for their friends, the availability of a particular cask ale, non-smoking or formerly as a place to smoke freely, or maybe a darts team or pool table.

A society with a particular interest in the traditional British beers and the preservation of the 'integrity' of the public house is the Campaign for Real Ale, (CAMRA).

HISTORY

The inhabitants of the British Isles have been drinking ale since the Bronze Age, but it was with the arrival of the Romans and the establishment of the Roman road network that the first inns, in which the weary traveller could obtain refreshment, began to appear. By the time the Romans left, the beginnings of the modern pub had been established. They became so commonplace that in 965 King Edgar decreed that there should be no more than one alehouse per village.

The Royal Standard of England, a pub near Beaconsfield, is a present-day survivor that grew from a Saxon alehouse. The Saxon alewife would put a green bush up on a pole to let people know her brew was ready. As well as strong ale, small ale was made. A traveller in the early Middle Ages could obtain overnight accommodation in monasteries, but later a demand for hostelries grew with the popularity of pilgrimages and travel. The Hostellers of London were granted guild status in 1446 and in 1514 the guild became the Worshipful Company of Innholders.

The interior of a typical English pub, showing three common features: the bar (left), an old-fashioned fireplace (left of centre), and a modern fruit machine (right)

Traditional English ale was made solely from fermented malt. The practice of adding hops to produce beer was introduced from the Netherlands in the early 15th century. Alehouses would each brew their own distinctive ale, but independent breweries began to appear in the late 17th century. By the end of the century almost all beer was brewed by commercial breweries.

The 18th century saw a huge growth in the number of drinking establishments, primarily due to the introduction of gin. Gin was brought to England by the Dutch after the Glorious Revolution of 1688 and started to become very popular after the government created a market for grain that was unfit to be used in brewing by allowing unlicensed gin production, whilst imposing a heavy duty on all imported spirits. As thousands of gin-shops sprang up all over England, brewers fought back by increasing the number of alehouses. By 1740 the production of gin had increased to six times that of beer and because of its cheapness it became popular with the poor leading to the so-called Gin Craze. Over half of the 15,000 drinking establishments in London were gin-shops. The drunkenness and resultant lawlessness created by gin was seen to lead to ruination and degradation of the working classes. The distinction was illustrated by William Hogarth in his engravings Beer Street and Gin Lane. The Gin Act (1736) imposed high taxes on retailers but led to riots in the streets. The prohibitive duty was gradually reduced and finally abolished in 1742. The 1751 Gin Act however was more successful. It forced distillers to sell only to licensed retailers and brought gin-shops under the jurisdiction of local magistrates.

LICENSING AND RECORDS

The Wine and Beerhouse Act 1869 re-introduced the stricter controls of the previous century. The sale of Beers, Wines or Spirits required a valuable licence for the premises from the local magistrates. A series of further provisions specifically regulated gaming, drunkenness, prostitution and other undesirable conduct on licensed premises, enforceable by prosecution or more effectively by the landlord under threat of forfeiting his licence. Licences were only granted, transferred or renewed at special Licensing Sessions courts, and were strictly limited to respectable individuals (initially often ex-servicemen or police). Licence conditions varied widely, according to local practice. They would specify permitted hours, which might require Sunday closing, or conversely permit all-night opening near a market. Typically they might require opening throughout the permitted hours, and the provision of food or lavatories. Once obtained, licences were jealously protected by the licensees (always individuals expected to be generally present, not a remote owner or company), and even "Occasional Licences" to serve drinks at temporary premises such as fêtes would usually be granted only to existing licensees. Objections might be made by the police, rival landlords or anyone else on the grounds of infractions such as serving drunks, disorderly or dirty premises, or ignoring permitted hours. However licensing was gradually liberalised after the 1960s, until contested licensing applications became very rare, and the remaining administrative function was transferred to Local Authorities in 2005.

Detailed records were kept on licensing, giving the Public House, its address, owner, licensee and misdemeanours of the licensees for periods often going back for hundreds of years. Many of these records survive and can be viewed, for example, at the London Metropolitan Archives centre.

By the end of the 18th century a new room in the pub was established: the saloon. Beer establishments had always provided entertainment of some sort-singing, gaming or a sport. Balls Pond Road in Islington was named after an establishment run by Mr Ball that had a pond at the rear filled with ducks, where drinkers could, for a certain fee, go out and take their chance at shooting the fowl. More common, however, was a card room or a billiards room. The saloon was a room where for an admission fee or a higher price of drinks, singing, dancing, drama or comedy was performed and drinks would be served at the table. From this came the popular music hall form of entertainment-a show consisting of a variety of acts. A most famous London saloon was the Grecian Saloon in The Eagle, City Road, which is still famous these days because of an English nursery rhyme: "Up and down the City Road / In and out The Eagle / That's the way the money goes / Pop goes the weasel.". The implication being that, having frequented The Eagle public house, the customer spent all his money, and thus needed to 'pawn' his 'weasel' to get some more. The exact definition of the 'weasel' is unclear but the two most likely definitions are: that a weasel is a flat iron used for finishing clothing; or that 'weasel' is cockney rhyming slang for a coat (weasel and stoat).

A few pubs have stage performances, such as serious drama, stand-up comedians, a musical band or striptease; the highly contentious juke box or "muzak" has otherwise replaced the musical tradition of a piano and singing.

By the 20th century, the saloon, or lounge bar, had settled into a middle class room-carpets on the floor, cushions on the seats, and a penny or two on the prices, while the public bar, or tap room, remained working class with bare boards, sometimes with sawdust to absorb the spitting, hard seats, and cheap beer.

Later, the public bars gradually improved until sometimes almost the only difference was in the prices, so that customers could choose between economy and exclusivity (or youth and age, or a juke box or dartboard). During the blurring of the class divisions in the 1960s and 70s, the distinction between the saloon and the public bar was often seen as archaic, and was frequently abolished, usually by the removal of the dividing wall or partition itself. While the names of Saloon and Public Bar may still be seen on the doors of pubs, the prices (and often the standard of furnishings and decoration) are the same throughout the premises, and many pubs now comprises one large room. However, the issues of smoking and eating encourage some pubs to maintain distinct rooms or areas, especially where the building requires it, and in a few pubs there still remain rooms or seats which by local custom "belong" to particular customers.

UK OPENING HOURS AND REGULATION

From the middle of the 19th century restrictions were placed on the opening hours of licensed premises in the UK. These culminated in the Defence of the Realm Act of August 1914, which, along with the introduction of rationing and the censorship of the press, also restricted the opening hours of public houses to 12noon-2.30pm and 6.30pm-9.30pm. Opening for the full licensed hours was compulsory, and closing time was equally firmly enforced by the police; a landlord might lose his licence for infractions. There was a special case established under the State Management Scheme where the brewery and licensed premises were bought and run by the state until 1973, most notably in the Carlisle District. During the twentieth century elsewhere, both the licensing laws and enforcement were progressively relaxed, and there were differences between parishes; in the 1960s, at closing time in Kensington at 10.30pm, drinkers would rush over the parish boundary to be in good time for "Last Orders" in Knightsbridge before 11pm, a tradition observed in many pubs adjoining licensing area boundaries. Some Scots and Welsh parishes remained officially "dry" on Sundays (although often this merely required knocking at the back door of the pub). However, closing times were increasingly disregarded in the country pubs. In England and Wales by 2000 pubs could legally open from 11am (12 noon on Sundays) through to 11 pm (10.30 pm on Sundays). That year was also the first to allow continuous opening for 36 hours from 11 am on New Year's Eve to 11 pm on New Year's Day. In addition, many cities had by-laws to allow some pubs to extend opening hours to midnight or 1 am, whilst nightclubs had long been granted late licences to serve alcohol into the morning.

Scotland's and Northern Ireland's licensing laws have long been more flexible, allowing local authorities to set pub opening and closing times. In Scotland, this stemmed out of a late repeal of the wartime licensing laws, which stayed in force until 1976.

The Licensing Act 2003, which came into force on November 24, 2005, aimed to consolidate the many laws into a single act. This now allows pubs in England and Wales to apply to the local authority for opening hours of their choice. This has proved controversial, with supporters arguing that it will end the concentration of violence around half past 11, when people must leave the pub, making policing easier. Critics have claimed that these laws will lead to '24-hour drinking'. By the day before the law came into force, 60,326 establishments had applied for longer hours, and 1,121 had applied for a licence to sell alcohol 24 hours a day. However, many argue that few of these establishments will be constantly open.

PUB GAMES AND SPORTS

Numerous traditional games are played in pubs, ranging from the well-known darts, skittles, dominoes, cards and bar billiards, to the more obscure Aunt Sally, Nine Men's Morris and ringing the bull. Betting is legally limited to certain games such as cribbage or dominoes, but these are now rarely seen. In recent decades the game of pool (both the British and American versions) has increased in popularity, other table based games such as snooker, Table Football are also common.

Increasingly, more modern games such as video games and slot machines are provided. Many pubs also hold special events, from tournaments of the aforementioned games to karaoke nights to pub quizzes. Some play pop music, or show football and rugby on big screen televisions. Despite the wide range of distractions now available in pubs, doing nothing other than drinking and talking remains perfectly acceptable. Shove ha'penny and Bat and trap was also popular in pubs south of London.

ENGLISH PUB FOOD

Traditionally pubs in England were drinking establishments and little emphasis was placed on the serving of food, usually called 'bar snacks'. The usual fare consisted of specialised English snack food such as pork scratchings, pickled eggs, along with crisps and peanuts-salted snacks sold or given away to increase customers' thirst. If a pub served meals they were usually basic dishes such as a ploughman's lunch. In South East England (especially London) it was common until recent times for vendors selling cockles, whelks, mussels and other shellfish, to sell to customers during the evening and at closing time. Many mobile shellfish stalls would set up near to popular pubs, a practice that continues in London's East End.

Recently (10-15 years), food has become much more important as part of a pub's trade and today most pubs serve lunches and dinners at the table (colloquially this is known in England as pub grub) in addition to (or instead of) snacks consumed at the bar: they may even have a separate dining room. Some pubs, serve excellent meals which can rival a good restaurant's and going for a 'pub lunch' can be a real treat-a pub which claims to focus on quality food (perhaps rather than necessarily on good beer) will now call itself a gastropub. The growth in importance of food, and the appeal of eating informally in a pub rather than with the good manners expected in a restaurant, has led to some establishments giving all tables over to food and removing the bar stools (even though a visitor expecting a quick drink and a conversation at the bar is likely to receive short shrift at such places, there is no legal bar to such a licensed restaurant calling itself a pub).

BRITISH PUB SIGNS

In 1393 King Richard II compelled landlords to erect signs outside their premises. The legislation stated "Whosoever shall brew ale in the town with intention of selling it must hang out a sign, otherwise he shall forfeit his ale." This was in order make them easily visible to passing inspectors of the quality of the ale they provided.

Another important factor was that during the Middle Ages a large percentage of the population would have been illiterate and so pictures were more useful than words as a means of identifying a public house. For this reason there was often no reason to write the establishment's name on the sign and inns opened without a formal written name-the name being derived later from the illustration on the public house's sign. In this sense, a pub sign can be thought of as an early example of visual branding.

The very earliest signs were often not painted but consisted, for example, of paraphernalia connected with the brewing process such as bunches of hops or brewing implements, which were suspended above the door of the public house. In some cases local nicknames, farming terms and puns were also used. Local events were also often commemorated in pub signs. Simple natural or religious symbols such as the 'The Sun', 'The Star' and 'The Cross' were also incorporated into pub signs, sometimes being adapted to incorporate elements of the heraldry (e.g. the coat of arms) of the local lords who owned the lands upon which the public house stood. Some pubs also have Latin inscriptions (see image). Other favourite subjects which lent themselves to visual depiction included the name of great battles (e.g. Trafalgar), explorers, local notables, discoveries, sporting heroes and members of the royal family. Some pub signs are in the form of a pictorial pun or rebus. For example, a pub in Crowborough, UK called The Crow and Gate has an image of a crow with gates as wings.

In the modern era most British pubs still have highly decorated signs hanging over their doors, and these retain their original function of enabling the rapid identification of the public house-a memorable and prominently located pub sign is still an important means of picking up passing trade. Today's pub signs almost always bear the name of the pub, both in words and in pictorial representation.

Pub Names

Farewell to the Nowhere Inn Particular.

- relating to its location: The Three Arrows, The Cross, The Railway, The Church

- reflecting local trades or related to the pub's clientele: The Mason's Arms, The Foresters, The Square and Compass
- ironic descriptions of the pub itself: the smallest pub in Britain is called The Nutshell
- local sporting activities: The Cricketers, The Fox and Hounds, The Fighting Cocks
- a noted individual: The Marquis of Granby, The Lord Nelson, The Emma Hamilton
- an historic event: The Trafalgar, The Royal Oak
- often incorporating the word 'Head'; The King's Head, The Queen's Head, The Sultan's Head
- alluding amusingly to everyday phrases: The Nowhere Inn Particular, The Dewdrop Inn, The Drift Inn (known locally as the "stagger oot"), Down The Hatch
- with a royal or aristocratic association: The Royal Standard, The King's Arms, The King's Head, The Queen Victoria, The Duke of Cambridge, The Anglesea Arms
- with the names of two objects which may or may not be complementary: The George and Dragon, The Goat and Compasses (humorous corruption of the puritan phrase "God encompass" of the 1600s in England), The Rose and Crown, The Dog and Handgun, The Elephant and Castle, The Crow and Gate, The Rummer and Grapes.
- The surname of its landlord, particularly in Ireland: O'Neill's, Tí hAnraí (Henry's house).
- with names of tools or products of trades: The Harrow, The Propeller, The Wheatsheaf
- with names of items, particularly animals, that may be part of a coat of arms (heraldic charges): The Red Lion, The Unicorn, The White Bear.

- with reference to history of the local area, for example The Strugglers in Lincoln refers to how people being publicly executed by hanging would struggle for air. Ironically the famous executioner Albert Pierrepoint was landlord of the Help the Poor Struggler at Hollinwood, near Oldham, for several years after WW2, and had to hang one of his own regulars, James Corbitt. Also Ye olde Trip to Jerusalem, (Nottingham, 1189), refers to its role as a resting place for the knights of Richard I on their way to the third crusade.

A very common name is the "Marquis of Granby". John Manners, Marquess of Granby was the son of John Manners, 3rd Duke of Rutland) and a general in the 18th century British Army. He showed a great concern for the welfare of his men, and on their retirement, provided funds for many of them to establish taverns, which were subsequently named after him.

Many names for pubs that appear nonsensical may have come from corruptions of older names or phrases, often producing a visual image to signify the pub. For example, the name The Goat and Compasses is a corruption of the phrase "God encompasseth us". These images had particular importance for identifying a pub on signs and other media before literacy became widespread. Another example of a mistaken pub name is the Oyster Reach pub in Ipswich, England. This pub spent several decades being called the Ostrich, before historians informed the owners of the original name. More possible but uncorroborated corruptions include "The Bag o'Nails" (Bacchanals), "Elephant and Castle", (Infanta de Castile) and "The Bull and Bush", which purportedly celebrates the victory of Henry VIII at "Boulougne Bouche" or Boulougne Harbour. While these corruptions are amusing there are usually more substantiated explanations available.

A too-obviously humorous name is likely to be a recent coining of a marketing executive, rather than traditional.

This is especially true for names with unsubtle double-entendres or names which have elements common to all the pubs in a particular chain (eg "XXXX and Firkin").

Tied Houses and Free Houses in Britain

After the development of the large London porter breweries in the 18th century, the trend grew for pubs to become tied houses which could only sell beer from one brewery (a pub not tied in this way was called a "Free House"). The usual arrangement for a tied house was that the pub was owned by the brewery but rented out to a private individual (landlord) who ran it as a separate business (even though contracted to buy the beer from the brewery). A growing trend in the late 20th century was for the brewery to run their pubs directly, employing a salaried manager (who perhaps could make extra money by commission, or by selling food).

Most such breweries, such as the regional breweries Shepherd Neame in Kent and Youngs in London, control hundreds of pubs in a particular region of the UK, whilst a few, such as Greene King, are spread nationally. The landlord of a tied pub may be an employee of the brewery-in which case he would be a manager of a managed house, or a self-employed tenant who has entered into a lease agreement with a brewery, a condition of which is the legal obligation (trade tie) only to purchase that brewery's beer. This tied agreement provides tenants with trade premises at a below market rent providing people with a low-cost entry into self-employment. The beer selection is mainly limited to beers brewed by that particular company. A Supply of Beer law, passed in 1989, was aimed at getting tied houses to offer at least one alternative beer, known as a guest beer, from another brewery. This law has now been repealed but while in force it has dramatically altered the whole industry and it is hard to see how the consumer has actually benefited from this change.

The period since the 1980's saw many breweries absorbed by, or becoming by take-overs, larger companies in the food, hotel or property sectors. The relatively low returns of a pub-owning business led to many breweries selling their pub estates, especially those in cities, often to a new generation of small chains, many of which have now grown considerably and have a national presence. Other chains, such as All Bar One and Pitcher and Piano offer youth-oriented atmospheres, often in premises larger than traditional pubs.

A free house is, strictly, simply a pub that is free of the control of any one particular brewery. But "Free" in this context does not necessarily mean "independent", and the view that "free house" on a pub sign is a guarantee of a quality, range or type of beer available is a mistake. Many free houses are not independent family businesses but are owned by large pub companies. In fact, these days there are very few truly free houses, either because a private pub owner has had to come to a financial arrangement with a brewer or other company in order to fund the purchase of the pub, or simply because the pub is owned by one of the large pub chains and pub companies (PubCos) which have sprung up in recent years. Some chains have rather uniform pubs and products, some allow managers some freedom. One of the largest pub chains does sell large amounts of a wide variety of real ale at low prices-but its pubs are not specifically "real ale pubs", being in the city centre to attract the Saturday night crowds and so also selling large quantities of alcopops and big-brand lager to large groups of young people.

British Pub Companies and Pub Chains

Organisations such as Wetherspoons and Eerie, were formed in the UK since changes in legislation in the 1980s necessitated the break-up of many larger tied estates. A PubCo is a company involved in the retailing but not the manufacture of beverages, while a pub chain may be run either by a PubCo or by a brewery. If the owning company is NOT a brewery, then the pub is technically a free house, however limited the manager is in his/her beer-buying choice. Pubs within a chain will usually have lots in common, such as fittings, promotions, ambience and range of food and drink on offer. A pub chain will position itself in the marketplace for a target audience. One company may run several pub chains aimed at different segments of the market. Pub chains are successful, though some people object that they do not reflect local history and customs. Pubs for use in a chain are bought and sold in large units, often from regional breweries which are then closed down. Newly acquired pubs are often renamed by the new owners, and many people resent the loss of traditional names, especially if their favourite regional beer disappears at the same time. A small number of pub chains (usually small ones) are noted for the independence they grant their managers, and hence the wide range of beers available.

Pubs in British Popular Culture

Inns and taverns feature throughout English literature and poetry, from Chaucer onwards. All the major soap operas on British television feature a pub, with their 'pub' becoming a household name. The Rovers Return is the pub on Coronation Street, the British 'soap' broadcast on ITV. The Queen Vic (short for the Queen Victoria) is the pub on EastEnders, the major 'soap' on BBC One, while The Bull in The Archers and the Woolpack on Emmerdale are also central meeting points. The sets of each of the three major television soap operas have been visited by royalty, including Queen Elizabeth II. The centrepiece of each visit was a trip into the Rovers, the Vic or the Woolpack to be offered a drink.

Much of the plotline in British film Shaun of the Dead involves the characters trying to reach their local public house, The Winchester, to escape a zombie invasion. Shaun (Simon Pegg) and Ed (Nick Frost) advocate the pub as the perfect location to wait for help because of their selection priorities: It must be (a) safe, (b) familiar, (c) someplace where Ed can smoke.

British comedian Al Murray's best-known character is a comic right-wing bigot, The Pub Landlord, not necessarily a faithful representation of the typical southern-English pub landlord.

US president George W. Bush fulfilled his ambition of visiting a 'genuine English pub' during his November 2003 state visit to the UK when he had lunch and a pint of non-alcoholic lager with British Prime Minister Tony Blair at the Dun Cow pub in Sedgefield, County Durham.

Pub Music

While many pubs now play piped pop music, the Pub has historically been a popular venue for live song. See:

- Pub rock
- Pub songs
- Folk music

The pub has also been celebrated in popular music. Examples are "Hurry Up Harry" by the 1970s punk rock act Sham 69, the chorus of which was the chant "We're going down the pub" repeated several times. Another such song is "Two Pints Of Lager and a Packet of Crisps Please!" by UK punk band Splodgenessabounds.

As a reaction against piped music, the Quiet Pub Guide was written, telling its readers where to go to avoid piped music.

THEME PUBS

Pubs that cater for a niche audience, such as sports fans or people of certain nationalities are known as theme pubs. Examples of theme pubs include sports bars, rock pubs, biker pubs, Goth pubs, strip pubs, and Irish pubs (see below).

In the U.S., almost all drinking establishments called "pubs" are simply bars with an Irish or British theme.

IRISH PUBLIC HOUSES

Superficially there is little difference between an Irish pub and its UK counterpart. However, closer scrutiny will reveal some differences. Pub frontages are generally plainer and less ornamented than their British counterparts are, and hanging signs are absent, with the name of the pub or proprietor being displayed above the door. The use of the term "bar" for a pub is more common in Ireland than in the UK.

The social and economic role of the pub in Ireland has changed considerably over the last century. Prior to the 1960s and the arrival of supermarket and grocery chains in the country; Irish pubs usually operated as a 'Spirit grocery', combining the running of pub with a grocery, hardware or other ancillary business on the same premises (in some cases, publicans also acted as undertakers, and this unusual combination is still common today in the Republic of Ireland). A well-known pub in Abbeyleix, Morrisey's, is representative of the traditional spirit grocers. Spirit groceries first appeared in the mid 18th Century, when a growing temperance movement in Ireland forced publicans to diversify their businesses to compensate for declining spirit sales. With the arrival of increased competition in the retail sector, many pubs lost the retail end of their business and concentrated solely on the licensed trade. Many pubs in Ireland still resemble grocer's shops of the 19th Century, with the bar counter and rear shelving taking up the majority of the space in the main bar area, apparently leaving little room for customers. This seemingly counterproductive arrangement is a design artefact dating from prior operation as a spirit grocery, and also accounts for the differing external appearance of English & Irish Pubs. Spirit Grocers in Northern Ireland were forced to choose between either the retail or the licensed trades upon the partition of Ireland in 1922, and this pub type can no longer be found there.

In contrast to England, Ireland's pubs usually bear the name of the current or a previous owner, e.g. Murphy's or O'Connor's, and traditional pub names are absent. Famous traditional pubs in Dublin which have the characteristics outlined above include O'Donoghue's, Doheny & Nesbitt's & the Brazen Head, which bills itself as Ireland's oldest pub (a distinction it shares with several other pubs). Some pubs are named after famous streets such Sober Lane in Cork which is named after Father Matthew's Hall of Abstinence. Individual pubs are also associated with famous Irish writers and poets such as Patrick Kavanagh, Brendan Behan and James Joyce.

Pubs in Northern Ireland are largely identical to their southern counterparts. A side effect of the 'Troubles' was that the lack of a tourist industry meant that a comparatively higher proportion of traditional bars have survived the wholesale refitting of Irish pub interiors in the English style in the 1950s and 1960s. This refitting was driven by the need to expand seating areas to accommodate the growing numbers of tourists, and was a direct consequence of the growing dependence of the Irish economy on tourism. Famous traditional pubs in Belfast include the National Trust's Crown Liquor Saloon, and the city's oldest bar, McHugh's. Outside Belfast, pubs such as the House of McDonnell in Ballycastle (a former spirit grocery retaining all the characteristics of the type) and Grace Neill's in Donaghadee are representative of the traditional country pub.

The pubs listed above are notable as being truly representative of the traditional Irish type (while some may have been expanded, the original bar areas have been retained in all cases), as few remain today after the extensive refitting noted above. The majority of 'traditional' pubs in Ireland today have been refurbished in a pastiche of the original style during the 1990s. Many Irish pubs were refurbished in this manner so as to increase their attractiveness to tourists by more closely resembling the 'Irish pubs' found outside Ireland; and thus have more in common with them (many were refurbished by the same outfitting companies) than the traditional pub type they purport to represent.

The sentimental image of Ireland held by many tourists and members of the Irish diaspora has also resulted in changes to the Irish pub experience in many areas. The notion that there is more live music in an Irish pub, and that a customer is more likely to entertain the assembly with a song is a myth created and actively promoted by the Irish tourist industry. Pubs of this type (so-called 'singing pubs') are more likely to be found in areas dependent on tourism such as the south-west of Ireland. These pubs are conspicuously absent in areas where tourism is not a major part of the local economy, such as the midlands or border counties. 'Singing pubs' are also absent from Northern Ireland. Pubs in tourist oriented areas are also more likely to serve food to their customers, a recent phenomenon dating from the 1970s. Prior to this time food was not served in the vast majority of Irish pubs, as eating out was uncommon in Ireland (except in "eating-houses" set up on market days) and most towns and villages had at least one commercial hotel where food was available throughout the day. The provision of meals in pubs since this time is largely the result of an effort by Irish publicans to capture an increased revenue stream from the tourist sector (where such revenue is available). The majority of traditional rural pubs not on the major tourist trails retain this characteristic and do not serve food; while traditional bars in urban areas such as Dublin, Armagh, Galway, and Sligo have responded to the increase in Irish people eating outside the home (a by-product of so called 'Celtic Tiger' economy during the 1990s); and now provide meals throughout the day.

The smoking ban in the Republic has noticeably changed the Irish pub experience; many pubs now offer enclosed and often heated outdoor smoking areas. While many people object, the greater majority of people appear content with the legislation, which came into effect in Northern Ireland in April 2007. Irish Pubs have been opened throughout the world, particularly in the 1980s and 1990s, from Boston to Frankfurt, Johannesburg to Beijing. While ubiquitous, they generally have little in common with pubs in Ireland.

The vast majority of pubs in Ireland are independently owned and licensed, or owned by a chain that does not have any brewery involvement, generally meaning that nearly every pub sells a similar but extensive range of products. Some microbreweries operate their own pubs or chains of pubs, where the range is more limited, with only their own products and a few others.

5

DISCOTHEQUE

INTRODUCTION

A discothèque (or discoteque), IPA is an entertainment venue or club with recorded music played by "Discaires" (Disc jockeys) through a PA system, rather than an on-stage band. The word derives from the French word discothèque (a type of nightclub). Discothèque is a portmanteau coined around 1941 from disc and bibliothèque (library) by La Discothèque, then located on the Rue de la Huchette in Paris, France (Jones + Kantonen, 1999). Previously, most bars and nightclubs used live bands as entertainment.

1970s and early 1980s

By the late 1970s many major US cities had thriving disco club scenes which were centered around discotheques, nightclubs, and private loft parties where DJs would play disco hits through powerful PA systems for the dancers. The DJs played "... a smooth mix of long single records to keep people "dancing all night long" " Some of the prestigious clubs had elaborate light organs, which converted audio signals into colored lights that throbbed to the beat of the music or even glass-floored dance floors with colored lights.

Some cities had disco dance instructors or dance schools which taught people how to do popular disco dances such as "touch dancing", the "hustle" and the "cha cha." There were also disco fashions that discotheque-goers wore for nights out at their local disco, such as sheer, flowing Halston dresses for women and shiny polyester Qiana shirts for men with pointy collars, preferably open at the chest, often worn with double-knit suit jackets.

2000s

Today the term discothèque is usually synonymous with nightclubs in France because disco music is still very popular there, but in contemporary English usage it is now very dated, because nightclubs have not been commonly called "discos" since the early 1980s. The term "disco" was originally a 1960s US abbreviation of discothèque, a place where "disco music" was played.

Some Historical Discothèques

- Ad Lib, in London, opened 1963 by Nicholas Luard and Lord Timothy Willoughby
- La Discothèque, in London, opened 1960
- Chez Regine, in Paris' Latin Quarter, opened 1957 by Régine
- La Discothèque, in Paris (on rue Hachette), opened 1941
- Whisky à Go-Go, in Paris, opened 1947 by Paul Pacine
- 2001 Odyssey, in Brooklyn, New York (was rechristened as The Spectrum in 1987; club demolished in late 2005)
- Arthur, in New York City, opened 1965 by Sybil Burton at site of the defunct El Morocco
- Aux Puces, in New York City, one of the first gay discos
- Cheetah, in New York City, at Broadway and 53rd Street
- Civic Theatre Disco in New Orleans owned and operated by Glen Tortorich. A converted Art Deco

theater was billed as the world's largest disco accommodating over 1500 and referred to as the Studio 54 of the South.

- Dlux club Caspe dlux.es
- Down The Street, in Asbury Park, New Jersey, open until 1999
- Electric Circus, opened 1967 on St. Mark's Place
- Il Mio (an Italian "discoteca"), in New York City,
- L'Interdit, in New York City
- La Dom, downstairs from Electric Circus; run by Andy Warhol
- Le Club, in New York City, opened 1960 by Olivier Coquelin, a French expatriate
- Ones Discotheque, New York City 1972-1982
- Peppermint Lounge, in New York City, opened 1961
- Shepheard's, in New York City,
- Studio 54, in New York City, which was notable for its sexuality, and was operated by Steve Rubell; depicted in the 1998 film 54; parodied in the 2002 movie Austin Powers in Goldmember as Studio 69.
- The Loft, in New York City, opened 1970 by David Mancuso
- The Sanctuary, in New York City, a famous early-1970s gay disco; part of the movie Klute was filmed there
- Whisky a Go Go, in Chicago
- Whisky a Go Go, in West Hollywood, California, opened 1964

DISCO

The term disco, which is a shortened form of discothèque, refers to a specific style of pop music that was derived in

U.S.A. from funk and soul, and to the dance styles popular in 1970s disco clubs (e.g., "The Hustle"). In Europe the same term used for the European Disco productions, that had 50s and 60s Europop influences. Later, those European productions (mostly Italian and German) were named "Euro Disco" and "Disco" was only used for the U.S.A. productions.

GAY BAR

A gay bar is a drinking establishment that caters exclusively or primarily to a gay and/or lesbian clientele. Other names include gay club or gay pub, queer bar, lesbian bar, dyke bar, or boy bar.

Gay bars range in size from the tiny, five-seat bars of Tokyo to large, multi-story "super-clubs" with several distinct areas and more than one dance floor. A large venue may be referred to as a nightclub, club, or bar, while smaller venues are typically called bars and sometimes pubs.

The only defining characteristic of a gay bar is the nature of its clientele. While many gay bars target the gay and / or lesbian communities, some (usually older and firmly established) gay bars have become gay, as it were, through custom, over a long period of time.

The serving of alcohol is the primary business of gay bars and pubs. Like non-gay establishments they serve as a meeting place and community focal point, in which conversation and relaxation is the primary focus of the clientele. Like other clubs, gay clubs are often advertised by handing out eye-catching flyers on the street, in gay or gay-friendly shops and venues, and at other clubs and events. These flyers frequently feature provocative images.

Music

Music, either live or, more commonly, mixed by a DJ or DJs, is often a prominent feature of gay bars. Music in gay bars, as in other bars, ranges in style from jazz and blues to disco, pop, drum and bass, punk, house, trance, and techno.

In the 1980s and early 1990s a particular genre of music distinct from the music being played by DJs in the mainstream or straight clubs at the same time, known as Hi-NRG or Eurobeat, became popular in gay bars and clubs. Some London, England clubs still distinguish themselves as gay clubs by the music they play, including the Royal Vauxhall Tavern in Vauxhall and Bromptons in Earls Court.

Characteristics and Amenities

Dance venues often feature elaborate lighting design and video projection, fog machines and raised dancing platforms. Hired dancers (called go-go girls or go-go boys) may also feature in decorative "cages" or on podiums.

Clientele are sometimes indiscriminate as to which restroom (men's or women's) they use, and this is widely tolerated in gay bars, though it may be illegal in some jurisdictions; unisex toilets are also common.

Some gay bars and clubs have backrooms, dimly lit rooms or corridors in which sexual activity takes place. This feature, once common, is now more unusual.

Gay bars and nightclubs are sometimes segregated by sex. In some establishments, people who are perceived to be of the "wrong" sex (for example, a man attempting to enter a women's club) may be unwelcome or even barred from entry. This may be more common in specialty bars, such as gay male leather fetish or BDSM bars, or bars or clubs which have a strict dress code.

It is also common in bars and clubs where sex on the premises is a primary focus of the establishment. On the other hand, gay bars are often welcoming of transgender and cross-dressed people, and drag shows are a common feature in many gay bars, even men-only spaces.

In the past lesbian-only bars were comparatively uncommon and tended to be concentrated in major urban conurbations. However they have experienced a resurgence in popularity. Some gay bars and clubs which have a predominantly male clientele, as well as some gay bathhouses and other sex clubs, may offer occasional women-only nights.

Some gay bars attempt to restrict entry only to gay or lesbian people, but in practice this is difficult to enforce. Most famously, Melbourne's Peel Hotel was granted an exemption from Australia's Equal Opportunities Act by a State tribunal, on the grounds that the exemption was needed to prevent "sexually-based insults and violence" aimed at the pub's patrons.

As a result of the decision, the pub is legally able to advertise as a "gay only" establishment, and door staff can ask people whether they are gay before allowing them inside, and can turn away non-gay people. The decision made world headlines and was widely decried.

History

The Stonewall Inn in New York City (January 2003), where a police raid in 1969 led to the Stonewall Rebellion, the beginning of the modern gay rights movement in America.

One of the oldest gay bars was the White Swan, on Vere Street, in London, England, which was raided in 1810 during the so-called Vere Street Coterie, leading to two executions-of Chandler Depenbrock and Keith Mangum-for the then crime of sodomy. The site was frequently the scene of gay marriages carried out by the Reverend John Church.

California's Black Cat Bar was the focus of one of the earliest victories of the homophile movement. In 1951 the California Supreme Court affirmed the right of homosexuals to assemble in a case brought by the heterosexual owner of the bar.

Stonewall Inn, located in Greenwich Village, New York City was the location of the Stonewall Riots of 1969, considered to be a major turning point of the modern gay rights movement in America.

Prior to the the riots, it was illegal in New York for a place serving alcoholic beverages to allow homosexuals to gather. The place could lose its liquor licence as a result. However, gay bars would often be tolerated--with strategic bribes given to the police.

NOTABLE GAY NIGHTCLUBS

Australia

- arq Nightclub, Sydney
- DIVA, Melbourne
- Heaven's Door Melbourne
- The Beat Brisbane
- The Columbian Hotel, Sydney
- The Family Brisbane
- The Imperial, Erskineville
- The Laird Melbourne
- The Market Hotel, Melbourne
- The Midnight Shift, Sydney
- The Oxford Tavern, Sydney
- The Xchange Hotel Melbourne
- Palms, Sydney
- The Sir Robert Peel Hotel ("The Peel") Melbourne
- Slide, Sydney
- Stonewall Hotel, Sydney

Czech Republic

- Drake's, Prague, official website

New Zealand

- Imerst, Wellington
- Bluenote Bar, Wellington
- Our Bar, Wellington
- Kamo, Auckland
- Urge, Auckland
- Supermarket, Auckland

Canada

- Woody's, Toronto
- Celebrities (Vancouver), Vancouver
- The Odyssey (Vancouver), Vancouver
- Diva's, Saskatoon
- The Roost, Edmonton

Costa Rica

- Club Oh!
- Bochinche

Denmark

- Pan Club Copenhagen (often just referred to as Pan) is the biggest gay club in Denmark.

Germany

- Berghain in Berlin, Germany

Hong Kong

- Volume New (opened November 2006) but hugely popular 'dancing bar'. Best known for it's music and international crowd. Their resident DJ Stonedog packs them in during his 'Hyper Handbag' Saturday night sets. Wednesdays they host a weekly 'New Arrivals' party where the locals welcome in flight crews, tourists and business travellers passing through the city each week.

Ireland

- The George in Dublin

Japan

- Advocates, Tokyo. A small bar with seating for fewer than five customers inside, customers at tables outside and spill out into Center Street. Known for its international customer base.

Philippines

- Adonis, Timog Ave. Quezon City, Philippines

Singapore

- Happy (Singapore)

United Kingdom

- Fire (nightclub), London.
- Heaven, London. Billing itself as "the world's most famous gay nightclub," has been open since 1979 and is underneath Charing Cross mainline train station
- G-A-Y, London. Based at the Astoria on Charing Cross Road. Claims to be the largest gay nightclub in Europe. It has two sister bars called G-A-Y Bar and G-A-Y Late which, together with G-A-Y, form a triangle in Soho.
- Black Cap, London. Long-established gay pub in Camden Town.
- Coleherne pub, Earls Court, London. Infamous haunt of serial killers Dennis Nilsen, Michael Lupo and Colin Ireland. Mentioned in Armistead Maupin's Tales of the City book Babycakes.

- Bromptons, London. Long-running gay venue on two floors with a dance floor and bar on the ground floor and a quieter cocktail bar on the upper floor.
- Profile, London. Owned and run by gay dating website Gaydar.
- Essential (nightclub), Manchester.
- Cruz (nightclub), Manchester.

United States

- Black Cat Bar, San Francisco, California (now closed).
- Stonewall Inn a gay bar in New York, New York the site of the Stonewall Riots in June 1969 that start of the gay rights movement in the USA.

6

THE RESTAURANT

INTRODUCTION

A restaurant is an establishment that serves prepared food and beverages to order, to be consumed on the premises. The term covers a multiplicity of venues and a diversity of styles of cuisine.

Restaurants are sometimes also a feature of a larger complex, typically a hotel, where the dining amenities are provided for the convenience of the residents and for the hotel to maximize their potential revenue. Such restaurants are often also open to non-residents.

A restaurant operator is called a restaurateur; both words derive from the French verb restaurer.

HISTORY

Food catering establishments which may be described as restaurants were known since the 12th century in Hangzhou, a cultural, political and economic center during China's Song Dynasty. With a population of over 1 million people, a culture of hospitality and a paper currency, Hangzhou was ripe for the development of restaurants. Ma Yu Ching's Bucket Chicken House, was established in Kaifeng, China, in 1153 AD, (though it should be noted this claim is not universally accepted--see the relevant Wikipedia article,) and is still serving up meals today. Probably growing out of the tea houses and taverns that catered to travellers, Hangzhou's restaurants blossomed into an industry catering to locals as well. Restaurants catered to different styles of cuisine, price brackets, and religious requirements. Even within a single restaurant much choice was available, an account from 1275 writes of Hangzhou restaurants:

"The people of Hangzhou are very difficult to please. Hundreds of orders are given on all sides: this person wants something hot, another something cold, a third something tepid, a fourth something chilled; one wants cooked food, another raw, another chooses roast, another grill".

In the West, whilst inns and taverns were known from antiquity, these were establishments aimed at travellers, and in general locals would rarely eat there. Restaurants, as businesses dedicated to the serving of food, and where specific dishes are ordered by the guest and generally prepared according to this order, emerged only in the 18th century. According to the Guinness Book of Records, the Sobrino de Botin in Madrid, Spain is the oldest restaurant in existence today. It opened in 1725. The term restaurant (from the French restaurer, to restore) first appeared in the 16th century, meaning "a food which restores", and referred specifically to a rich, highly flavoured soup. It was first applied to an eating establishment in around 1765 founded by a Parisian soup-seller named Boulanger. The first restaurant in the form that became standard (customers sitting down with individual portions at individual tables, selecting food from menus, during fixed opening hours) was the Grand Taverne de Londres ("the Great Tavern of London"), founded in Paris in 1782 by a man named Antoine Beauvilliers, a leading culinary writer and gastronomic authority who achieved a reputation as a successful restaurateur and later wrote what became a standard cook book L'Art du cuisinier (1814).

Restaurants became commonplace in France after the French Revolution broke up catering guilds and forced the aristocracy to flee, leaving a retinue of servants with the skills to cook excellent food; whilst at the same time numerous provincials arrived in Paris with no family to cook for them. Restaurants were the means by which these two could be brought together-and the French tradition of dining out was born.

A leading restaurant of the Napoleonic era was the Véry which was lavishly decorated, and boasted a menu with extensive choices of soups, fish and meat dishes, and scores of side dishes. Balzac often dined edaciously there. Although absorbed by a neighbouring business in 1869, the resulting establishment Le Grand Véfour is still in business in the 21st century.

The restaurant described by Britannica as the most illustrious of all those in Paris in the 19th century was the Café Anglais (the "English coffee-shop") on the Boulevard des Italiens, showing for a second time the high regard that Parisians evidently had for London, England, and the English-at least when it came to naming their restaurants.

Restaurants then spread rapidly across the world, with the first in the United States (Jullien's Restarator) opening in Boston in 1794. Most however continued on the standard approach (Service à la française) of providing a shared meal on the table to which customers would then help themselves, something which encouraged them to eat rather quickly. The modern formal style of dining, where customers are given a plate with the food already arranged on it, is known as Service à la russe, as it is said to have been introduced to France by the Russian Prince Kurakin in the 1810s, from where it spread rapidly to England and beyond.

TYPES OF RESTAURANTS

Restaurants range from unpretentious lunching or dining places catering to people working nearby, with simple food served in simple settings at low prices, to expensive establishments serving refined food and wines in a formal setting. In the former case, customers usually wear casual clothing. In the latter case, depending on culture and local traditions, customers might wear semi-casual, semi-formal, or even in rare cases formal wear.

Typically, customers sit at tables, their orders are taken by a waiter, who brings the food when it is ready, and the customers pay the bill before leaving. In finer restaurants there will be a host or hostess or even a maître d'hôtel to welcome customers and to seat them. Other staff waiting on customers include busboys and sommeliers.

Restaurants often specialize in certain types of food or present a certain unifying, and often entertaining, theme. For example, there are seafood restaurants, vegetarian restaurants or ethnic restaurants. Generally speaking, restaurants selling "local" food are simply called restaurants, while restaurants selling food of foreign origin are called accordingly, for example, a Chinese restaurant and a French restaurant..

Depending on local customs and the establishment, restaurants may or may not serve alcoholic beverages. Restaurants are often prohibited from selling alcohol without a meal by alcohol sale laws; such sale is considered to be activity for bars, which are meant to have more severe restrictions. Some restaurants are licensed to serve alcohol ("fully licensed"), and/or permit customers to "bring your own" alcohol (BYO / BYOB).

Specific Types of Restaurants

Types of restaurants include:

- Brasserie, bistro, pub
- Dining car
- Fast-food restaurant
- Family style restaurant

Restaurant Guides

Restaurant guides list the best places to eat. In 12th century Hanzhou (mentioned above as the location of the first restaurant,) signs could often be found posted in the city square listing the restaurants in the area and local customer's opinions of the quality of their food. This was an occasion for bribery and even violence. Today, restaurant review is carried out in a more civilized manner. One of the most famous contemporary guides, in Western Europe, is the Michelin series of guides which accord from 1 to 3 stars to restaurants they perceive to be of high culinary merit. Restaurants with stars in the Michelin guide are formal, expensive establishments; in general the more stars awarded, the higher the prices.

In the United States, the Mobil Travel Guides and the AAA rate restaurants on a similar 1 to 5 star (Mobil) or diamond (AAA) scale. Three, four, and five star/diamond ratings are roughly equivalent to the Michelin one, two, and three star ratings while one and two star ratings typically indicate more casual places to eat. In 2005, Michelin released a New York City guide, its first for the United States. The popular Zagat Survey compiles individuals' comments about restaurants but does not pass an "official" critical assessment. The Good Food Guide, published by the Fairfax Newspaper Group in Australia, is the Australian guide listing the best places to eat. Chefs Hats are awarded for outstanding restaurants and range from one hat through three hats. The Good Food Guide also incorporates guides to bars, cafes and providers.

Nearly all major American newspapers employ restaurant critics and publish on-line dining guides for the cities they serve. A few papers maintain a reputation for thorough and thoughtful review of restaurants to the standard of the good published guides, but others provide more of a listings service.

More recently Internet sites have started up that publish both food critic reviews and popular reviews by the general public. This is a growing area and the market is still immature with no sites yet gaining dominant public or critical support.

Economics

In economics, restaurants are the end of the supply chain in the foodservice industry. There is usually much competition in most cities since barriers to entry are relatively low, which means that for most restaurants, it is hard to make a profit. In most First World industrialized countries, restaurants are heavily regulated to ensure the health and safety of the customers.

The typical restaurant owner faces many obstacles to success, including raising initial capital, finding competent and skilled labour, maintaining consistent and excellent food quality, maintaining high standards of safety, and the constant hassle of minimising potential liability for any food poisoning or accidents that may occur.

Additionally, when economic conditions change-for example an increase in gasoline prices-households typically spend less on dining out.

In 2006, there are approximately 215,000 full-service restaurants in the United States, accounting for $298 billion, and approximately 250,000 limited-service (fast food) restaurants, accounting for $260 billion, according to the 2006 U.S. Industry & Market Outlook by Barnes Reports.

AUTOMAT

An Automat is a fast food restaurant where simple foods and drink are served by coin-operated and bill-operated vending machines. Originally, the machines took only nickels but modern automat vending machines accept bills. In the original format, a cashier would sit in a change booth in the center of the restaurant, behind a wide marble counter with five to eight rounded depressions in it. She would serve many customers at once, taking their money from the depressions and dropping nickels in its place. The diner would insert the required number of coins and then slide open a window to remove the meal, which was generally wrapped in waxed paper. The machines were filled from the kitchen behind. While most automats have since closed, a few still exist today, such as a New York City automat that opened in 2006 and a number that still exist in The Netherlands.

Unlike modern vending machines, food was served on real crockery with metal utensils, and drinks in glasses.

Inspired by the Quisiana Automat in Berlin, the first automat in the U.S. was opened June 12, 1902 at 818 Chestnut St. in Philadelphia by Horn & Hardart. The automat was brought to New York City in 1912 and gradually became part of popular culture in northern industrial cities. Horn & Hardart was the most prominent automat chain.

The format was threatened by the growth of suburbs and the rise of fast food restaurants catering to cars (with their drive-thru windows) in the 1950s; by the 1970s their remaining appeal was strictly nostalgic. Another contributing factor to their demise was undoubtedly the inflation of the 1960s and 70s, making the food too expensive to be bought conveniently with coins, and in a time before bill acceptors commonly appeared on vending equipment.

Another form of the Automat was used on some passenger trains, the last United States example being an Automat car on Amtrak's short-lived service to Janesville, Wisconsin in 2001. These were limited by mechanical problems, since the machines weren't necessarily intended for the bumpy ride on the rails, and state laws that prohibited alcoholic beverages from being sold by a machine. The automat food format is still popular in some other countries. For example, FEBO stores in The Netherlands, where the automat is called Automatiek, provide a variety of burgers, sandwiches, and krokets in vending machines that are back-loaded from a kitchen.

CAFÉ

A café (also spelled cafe, pronunciation (help info) IPA: ['kæfe?] or [kæ'fe?]) is a type of cafeteria, often with an enclosed or outdoor section extending onto the pavement or sidewalk, where food and drink are served. Generally serving coffee and other beverages, cafés (or more commonly known as cafeterias) also serve meals but this is generally not considered their main trade (in contrast to a restaurant).

The term can also refer to a coffee-house, tea room, lunchroom, bistro or a room in a hotel or restaurant where coffee and liquors are served. In the Netherlands, a café is an establishment selling liquor, as opposed a coffee-shop, which sells soft drugs (cannabis) and is typically not allowed to sell liquor.

Etymology, Spelling, and Pronunciation of Café

The most common English spelling, café, is the French spelling, and was adopted by English-speaking countries in the late 19th century. As English generally makes little use of diacritical marks, anglicisation involves a natural tendency to forgo them, and the anglicized spelling cafe has thus become very common in English-language usage throughout the world (although orthographic proscriptivists often disapprove of it). The Italian spelling, caffè, is also sometimes used in English.. In southern England, especially around London in the 1950s, the French pronunciation was often shortened to [kæf] and spelt caff.

The English words coffee and café both descend from the continental European translingual word root /kafe/, which appears in many European languages with various naturalized spellings, including Italian (caffè); Spanish (café); French (café); German (Kaffee); and others. European awareness of coffee (the plant, its seeds, the beverage made from the seeds, and the shops that sell the beverage) came through Europeans' contact with Turkey, and the Europeans borrowed both the beverage and the word root from the

Turks, who got them from the Arabs. The Arabic name qhawa was transformed into kaweh (strength, vigor) in the Ottoman Empire, and it spread from there to Europe, probably first through the Mediterranean languages (Italian, Spanish, French) and thence to German, English, and others.

CAFETERIA

A cafeteria is a type of food service location in which there is no table service, whether a restaurant or within an institution such as a large office building or school; a school dining location is also referred to as a canteen or dining hall. Cafeterias are different from coffee-houses, although that is the Spanish origin of the American word.

Instead of table service, there are food-serving counters/ stalls, either in a line or allowing arbitrary walking paths. Customers take the food they require as they walk along, placing it on a tray. In addition, there are often stations where customers order food and wait while it is prepared, particularly for items such as hamburgers or tacos which must be served hot and can be quickly prepared. Sometimes, for some food items and drinks, customers collect an empty container, pay at the check-out, and fill the container after the check-out. Free second servings are often allowed under this system. For legal purposes (and the consumption patterns of customers), this system is rarely or never used for alcoholic beverages.

Customers are either charged a flat rate for admission (as in a buffet), or pay at the check-out for each item.

As cafeterias require few employees, they are often found within a larger institution, catering to the clientele of that institution. For example, schools, colleges and their residence halls, department stores, hospitals, museums, and office buildings often have cafeterias.

At one time, cafeteria-style restaurants dominated the culture of the Southern United States, and to a lesser extent the Midwest. There were several prominent chains of them: Bickford's, Morrison's Cafeteria, Apple House, K&W, Britling, and Blue Boar among them.

There were also a number of smaller chains, usually in and around a single city. These institutions, with the exception of K&W, went into a decline in the 1960s with the rise of fast food and were largely finished off in the 1980s by the rise of "casual dining". A few chains-notably Luby's and Piccadilly Cafeterias (which took over the Morrison's chain), continue to fill some of the gap left by the decline of the older chains. Many of the smaller Midwestern chains, such as MCL Cafeterias centered around Indianapolis, are still very much in business.

History

The cafeteria as it is known in the United States originated in Los Angeles in the very late 19th century. It derives from earlier food service traditions brought to California from Mexico by immigrants. The name Cafeteria is in fact Spanish, and roughly means "coffee shop." In California the self-service style became more streamlined, with probable influence from the factory assembly lines coming into vogue at that time, and American-style foods were served, although in California cafeterias (restaurant and institutional iterations both) Mexican style dishes continued to be available alongside standard American fare. In the early 20th Century dozens of cafeterias stood in Los Angeles. Today, Clifton's Cafeteria is the only remaining cafeteria from that era. It opened in 1935 and is decorated to resemble a mountain wonderland in the manner of Yosemite National Park.

Other Countries

A cafeteria in Australia is called a canteen and is not set up like in the US. Service is much more like a takeaway store with patrons approaching a counter and ordering food, and paying at the register. This is in contrast to the US where the payment is usually included in their workplace/ school.

Other Names

A cafeteria in a U.S. military installation is known as either a chow hall, a mess hall, or, more correctly, a dining facility, whereas in common British armed forces parlance, it is known as a cookhouse or mess. Some monasteries and boarding schools refer to their cafeteria as a refectory. Students in the USA often refer to cafeterias as lunchrooms, though breakfast as well as lunch is often eaten there. Cafeterias serving university dormitories are sometimes called dining halls, dining commons, the "DC", or just "caf". A food court is a type of cafeteria found in many shopping malls and airports featuring multiple food vendors or concessions, although a food court could equally be styled as a type of restaurant as well, being more aligned with public, rather than institutionalised, dining.

College Cafeteria

A college cafeteria is a term in the United States that denotes a cafeteria that is designed to serve college students at the university. Also see the different meanings of the word college around the Anglosphere. These cafeterias can be a part of a residence hall or in a separate building. Many of these colleges employ their own students to work in the cafeteria. The amount of meals served to students varies from school to school, but is normally around 20 meals per week. Like normal cafeterias, a person will have a tray to select the food that they want, but instead of paying money, they pay beforehand by purchasing a meal plan.

The method of payment for college cafeterias is commonly in the form of a meal plan, whereby the patron pays a certain amount at the start of the semester and the details of the plan are stored on a computer system. Student ID cards are then used to access the meal plan. A meal plan is not necessary to eat at a college cafeteria however. Meal plans can vary widely in their details to best fit the needs of the students. Typically, the college tracks the student's usage of their plan by counting either the number of pre-defined meal servings, points, dollars, or number of buffet dinners. The plan may give the student a certain number of any of the above per week or semester and they may or may not roll over to the next week or semester.

Many schools offer several different options for using their meal plans. The main cafeteria is usually where most of the meal plan is used but smaller cafeterias, cafés, restaurants, bars, or even fast food chains located on campus may accept meal plans. A college cafeteria system often has a virtual monopoly on the students due to an isolated location or a requirement that residence contracts include a full meal plan. It is not uncommon for the entire food service operation to be outsourced to a managed services company such as Aramark, Sodexho and Compass Group (under the Scolarest name in the United Kingdom).

DESTINATION RESTAURANT

A destination restaurant is a restaurant with a chef or cuisine famous enough to be the reason patrons travel to a locale to experience the restaurant. In Europe, such a restaurant might be a Michelin Guide 3-star restaurant, which according to the guide is "worthy of a journey." There are typically 20-25 such restaurants in a country such as France.

In the United States, destination restaurants are typically among the country's best. They are often located outside of major metropolitan centers and rely on their renown to draw patrons. Destination restaurants often serve multi-course, prix fixe menus. Because of the complexity of the food and the large staffs, prices can be high.

The 2006 book, "National Geographic Passport to the Best--The 10 Best of Everything: an Ultimate Guide for Travellers," lists their choice of the world's ten best destination restaurants:

1. The Herbfarm, Woodinville, Washington USA
2. The French Laundry, Yountville, California USA
3. Chez Panisse, Berkeley, California USA
4. El Bulli, Girona, Spain
5. The Inn at Little Washington, Washington, Virginia USA
6. Fearrington House, Pittsboro, North Carolina USA
7. Le Jardin du Russie, Rome, Italy
8. Gambero Rosso, Tuscany, Italy
9. Whampoa Club, Shanghai, China
10. Wildfire Restaurant, Sydney, Australia

Examples

Europe

- L'Auberge de l'Ill, Illhaeusern, France
- El Bulli, Montjoi, Spain
- The Fat Duck, Bray, Berkshire, United Kingdom
- Jamie Oliver's restaurant, Fifteen, London, United Kingdom

North America

- The Breakwater Inn & Spa-Stripers, Kennebunkport, Maine
- The French Laundry, Yountville, California
- Sooke Harbour House, Sooke, British Columbia
- The Herbfarm, Woodinville, Washington
- The Inn at Little Washington, Washington, Virginia

- The Left Bank, Colorado, Vail. Famous for having Jean-Michel Chelain as chef.
- The White Barn, Kennebunkport, Maine
- Eigensinn Farm, Singhampton, Ontario, Canada
- Lumiere, Vancouver, British Columbia. Famous for having Rob Feenie as chef.

FAST FOOD RESTAURANTS

In the U.S., fast-food restaurants and take-outs have become so widespread that the traditional standard type is now sometimes referred to as a sit-down restaurant (a retronym). A common feature of fast food restaurants is a lack of cutlery or crockery, the customer is expected to eat the food directly from the disposable container it was served in using their hands.

There are various types of fast-food restaurant:

- one collects food from a counter and pays, then sits down and starts eating (self-service restaurant); sub-varieties:
    - one collects ready portions
    - one serves oneself from containers
    - one is served at the counter
- a special procedure is that one first pays at the cash desk, collects a ticket and then goes to the food counter, where one gets the food in exchange for the ticket
- one orders at the counter; after preparation the food is brought to one's table; paying may be on ordering or after eating.

Family Style

"Family style", or sometimes called table d'hôte ("host's table") in France, are restaurants that have a fixed menu and fixed price, usually with diners seated at a communal table such as on bench seats. More common in the 19th and early 20th century, they can still be found in rural communities, or as theme restaurants, or in vacation lodges. There is no menu to choose from, rather food is brought out in courses, usually with communal serving dishes, like at a family meal. Typical examples can include crabhouses, German-style beer halls, BBQ restaurants, hunting lodges. Some normal restaurants will mix elements of family style, such as a table salad or bread bowl that is included as part of the meal.

Casual Dining

A casual dining restaurant is a restaurant that serves moderately-priced food in a casual atmosphere. Except for buffet-style restaurants, casual dining restaurants typically provide table service. Casual dining comprises a market segment between fast food establishments and fine dining restaurants (see also Fast casual restaurant). In the United States, the bill per diner at a casual dining restaurant usually averages $10-$30 for an evening meal and slightly less for lunch, as of 2004.

Casual Dining versus Family Restaurant

Some casual dining restaurants serve beer or wine with meals or include a bar where alcoholic beverages are served, but they are generally distinct from drinking establishments. A casual dining restaurant that does not serve alcohol is often referred to as a family restaurant.

Fine Dining

Fine dining is a phrase used to describe restaurants that create a serious dining experience. The experience can start with the location and the view. The interior of such restaurants is often purported to be quite elegant and designed in accordance with the restaurant's concept. Service attempts to be impeccable, with chefs and service crew typically hailing from the best culinary schools.

Restaurants fitting the fine dining label are normally highly rated; in the four star range and will provide more nuanced service and more expensive food than a standard sit-down restaurant.

Fast Casual Dining

A fast casual restaurant is a type of restaurant which is similar to a fast-food restaurant in that it does not offer full table service, but promises a somewhat higher quality of food and atmosphere. It is a growing concept to fill the space between fast-food and casual dining.

Counter service accompanied by handmade food (often visible via an open kitchen) is typical. Alcohol may be served. Dishes like steak, which require experience on the part of the cook to get right, may be offered.

The menu is usually limited to an extended over-counter display, and options in the way the food is prepared are emphasized. Health-conscious items have a larger than normal portion of the menu, and some restaurants may emphasize high quality ingredients like free range chicken and freshly made salsas; Overall, the quality of the food is presented as much higher than conventional factory-made fast food. While full table service is not offered, conveniences like non-plastic utensils and plates are common.

The moderate volume music and nontraditional decor pioneered by Starbucks are fully embraced by fast casual restaurants-approximately half of the customers eat in the establishment, compared with a quarter of fast food customers.

Technomic Information Services created the term "fast casual restaurants" to describe restaurants with the following classifications:

- Limited-service or self-service format
- Average check between $6 and $9

- Made-to-order food with more complex flavors than fast food restaurants
- Upscale or highly developed decor....

Brasserie, Bistro, Pub

In France, a brasserie is a café doubling as a restaurant and serving single dishes and other meals in a relaxed setting. A bistro is a familiar name for a café serving moderately priced simple meals in an unpretentious setting, especially in Paris; bistros have become increasingly popular with tourists. Mainly in the UK and other countries influenced by British culture, the pub (short for public house) today serves a similar dual menu, offering beer and other alcohol along with basic food fare. Traditionally, pubs were primarily drinking establishments, whereas the modern pub business relies on food as well, to the point where gastropubs are known for their high-quality "pub food".

Dining Car

A dining car (British English: restaurant car) or diner (but not "diner car," except in uninformed parlance) is a railroad passenger car that serves meals on a train in the manner of a full-service, sit-down restaurant. It is distinct from other types of railroad food-service cars that do not duplicate the full-service restaurant experience, principally cars of various types in which one purchases food from a walk-up counter to be consumed either within the car or elsewhere in the train. While dining cars are less common today than they were in the past, they still play a significant role in passenger railroading, especially on medium-and long-distance trains.

FAST FOOD

Fast food is food cooked in bulk and in advance and kept warm, or reheated to order. Many fast-food restaurants, (also known as "Quick Service Restaurants" or QSR) are part of restaurant chains or franchise operations, and standardized foodstuffs are shipped to each restaurant from central locations. There are also simpler fast-food outlets, such as stands or kiosks, which may or may not provide shelter or chairs for customers.

Because the capital requirements to start a fast-food restaurant are relatively small, particularly in areas with non-existent or poorly enforced health codes, small individually-owned fast-food restaurants have become common throughout the world. Restaurants such as Culver's and Noodles, where the customers sit down and have their food orders brought to them, are also considered fast food.

History

Although fast-food restaurants are often viewed as a representation of a day by day family outing, the concept of "ready-cooked food to go" is as old as cities themselves; unique variations are historical in various cultures. Ancient Roman cities had bread-and-olive stands, East Asian cultures feature noodle shops. Flat bread and falafel are ubiquitous in the Middle East. Popular Indian "fast" food delicacies include Vada pav, Papri Chaat, Bhelpuri, Panipuri and Dahi Vada. In the French-speaking nations of West Africa, meanwhile, roadside stands in and around the larger cities continue to sell-as they have done for generations-a range of ready-to-eat, chargrilled meat sticks known locally as "brochettes" (not to be confused with the bread snack of the same name found in Europe).

Fast Food in America

The modern history of fast-food in America began on July 7, 1912 with the opening of a fast food restaurant called the Automat in New York. The Automat was a cafeteria with its prepared foods behind small glass windows and coin-operated slots. Joseph Horn and Frank Hardart had already opened an Automat in Philadelphia, but their "Automat" at

Broadway and 13th Street, in New York City, created a sensation. Numerous Automat restaurants were quickly built around the country to deal with the demand. Automats remained extremely popular throughout the 1920 s and 1930's.

The company also popularized the notion of "take-out" food, with their slogan "Less work for Mother". The American company White Castle is generally credited with opening the second fast-food outlet in Wichita, Kansas in 1921, selling hamburgers for five cents apiece. Among its innovations, the company allowed customers to see the food being prepared. White Castle later added five holes to each beef patty to increase its surface area and speed cooking times. White Castle was successful from its inception and spawned numerous competitors.

McDonald's

McDonald's, the largest fast-food chain in the world and the brand most associated with the term "fast food," was founded as a barbecue drive-in in 1940 by Dick and Mac McDonald. After discovering that most of their profits came from hamburgers, the brothers closed their restaurant for three months and reopened it in 1948 as a walk-up stand offering a simple menu of hamburgers, french fries, shakes, coffee, and Coca-Cola, served in disposable paper wrapping. As a result, they were able to produce hamburgers and fries constantly, without waiting for customer orders, and could serve them immediately; hamburgers cost 15 cents, about half the price at a typical diner.

Their streamlined production method, which they named the "Speedee Service System" was influenced by the production line innovations of Henry Ford. The McDonalds' stand was the milkshake machine company's biggest customer and a milkshake salesman named Ray Kroc travelled to California to discover the secret to their high-volume burger-and-shake operation. Kroc thought he could expand their concept, eventually buying the McDonalds' operation outright in 1961 with the goal of making cheap, ready-to-go hamburgers, french fries and milkshakes a nationwide business.

Kroc was the mastermind behind the rise of McDonald's as a national chain. The first part of his plan was to promote cleanliness in his restaurants. Kroc often took part at his own Des Plaines, Illinois, outlet by hosing down the garbage cans and scraping gum off the cement. Kroc also added great swaths of glass which enabled the customer to view the food preparation.

This was very important to the American public which became quite germ conscious. A clean atmosphere was only part of Kroc's grander plan which separated McDonald's from the rest of the competition and attributes to their great success. Kroc envisioned making his restaurants appeal to families of suburbs. "Where White Tower (one of the original fast food restaurants) had tied hamburgers to public transportation and the workingman...McDonald's tied hamburgers to the car, children, and the family." (Levinstein, p.228-229)

Wendy's

Wendy's, which was opened in Columbus, Ohio in 1969 by Dave Thomas, a protégé of Kentucky Fried Chicken founder Col. Harlan Sanders, is credited with pioneering the use of the "drive-thru" window to allow consumers to purchase fast food without having to park or exit their cars; it was first introduced in 1972, and copied by McDonald's in 1975.

Service

Fast-food outlets are take-away or take-out providers, often with a "drive-thru" service which allows customers to order and pick up food from their cars; but most also have a seating area in which customers can eat the food on the premises.

Nearly from its inception, fast food has been designed to be eaten "on the go" and often does not require traditional cutlery and is eaten as a finger food. Common menu items at fast food outlets include fish and chips, sandwiches, pitas, hamburgers, fried chicken, french fries, chicken nuggets, tacos, pizza, and ice cream, although many fast-food restaurants offer "slower" foods like chili, mashed potatoes, and salads.

Traditional Retail Outlets

Many petrol/gas stations have convenience stores which sell pre-packed sandwiches, donuts, and hot food. Many gas stations in the United States also sell frozen foods and have microwaves on the premises in which to prepare them.

Supermarkets often include their own cafes with prepared food service counters. Many markets prepare baked or rotisserie chickens due to the low cost of fowl and ease of preparation. Some, like ASDA and Wal-Mart may even include a well-known fast food chain within their own store, such as McDonald's or Subway.

Street Vendors and Concessions

Traditional street food is available around the world, usually from small operators and independent vendors operating from a cart, table, or portable grill. Common examples include Vietnamese noodle vendors, Middle Eastern falafel stands and New York City hot dog carts.

Food Preparation

The common preparation practice for small vendors consists of serving a few basic ingredients and toppings that can be cooked in batches and served quickly on the spot.

Modern commercial fast food, by contrast, is often highly processed and prepared in an industrial fashion, i.e., on a large scale with standard ingredients and standardised cooking and production methods. It is usually rapidly served in cartons or bags or in a plastic wrapping, in a fashion which minimizes cost. In most fast food operations, menu items are generally made from processed ingredients prepared at a central supply facility and then shipped to individual outlets where they are reheated, cooked (usually by microwave or deep-frying) or assembled in a short amount of time. This process ensures a consistent level of product quality, and is key to being able to deliver the order quickly to the customer and eliminate labor and equipment costs in the individual stores.

Pre-processed Ingredients and Nutritional Value

Because of commercial emphasis on speed, uniformity and low cost, fast food products are often made with ingredients formulated to achieve a certain flavor or consistency and to preserve freshness. Hydrogenated vegetable oils are pumped into fast foods which contain high amounts of trans fat. This requires a high degree of food engineering, the use of additives and processing techniques substantially alter the food from its original form and reduce its nutritional value.

BUSINESS

Consumer Spending

In the United States alone, consumers spent about US$110 billion on fast food in 2000 (which increased from US$6 billion in 1970). The National Restaurant Association forecasts that fast-food restaurants in the U.S. will reach US$142 billion in sales in 2006, a 5% increase over 2005. In comparison, the full-service restaurant segment of the food industry is expected to generate $173 billion in sales. Fast food has been losing market share to so-called fast casual restaurants, which offer more robust and expensive cuisines.

McDonald's and other Major Brands

McDonald's, a noted fast-food supplier, opened its first franchised restaurant in the US in 1955 (1974 in the UK).

It has become a phenomenally successful enterprise in terms of financial growth, brand-name recognition, and worldwide expansion. Ray Kroc, who bought the franchising license from the McDonald brothers, pioneered many concepts which emphasized standardization. He introduced uniform products, identical in all respects at each outlet, to increase sales. At the same time, Kroc also insisted on cutting food costs as much as possible, eventually using the McDonald's Corporation's size to force suppliers to conform to this ethos.

Other prominent international fast food companies include Burger King, the number two hamburger chain in the world, known for promoting its customized menu offerings (Have it Your Way); Wendy's, the number three burger chain and creator of the Drive thru concept; Dunkin' Donuts, a New England based chain that emphasized and refined the commissary model of food preparation; Starbucks, specializing in high-end fast food; KFC, a part of the largest restaurant chain in the world, Yum! Brands; and Dominos Pizza, a pizza chain known for popularizing home delivery of fast food.

Regional Chains

Many fast food operations have more local and regional roots, such as White Castle in the Midwest United States, along with Hardee's (owned by CKE Restaurants, which also owns Carl's Jr., whose locations are primarily on the United States West Coast), Krystal, Bojangles', and Zaxby's restaurants in the American Southeast, Raising Cane's in Louisiana, the famous In-N-Out Burger (in California, Arizona, and Nevada) and Tommy's chains in Southern California, Dick's Drive-In in Seattle Washington, and Arctic Circle in Utah and other western states. Also, Whataburger is a popular burger chain in the South and Mexico. Canada pizza chains Toppers Pizza and Pizza Pizza are primarily located in Ontario. Coffee chain Country Style operates only in Ontario, and competes with the famous coffee and donut chain Tim Hortons and Dunkin Donuts.

International Chains

The fast-food industry is popular in the United States, the source of most of its innovation, and many major international chains are based there. Seen as symbols of US dominance and perceived cultural imperialism, American fast-food franchises have often been the target of Anti-globalization protests and demonstrations against the US government. In 2005, for example, rioters in Karachi, Pakistan, who were initially angered because of the bombing of a Shiite mosque, destroyed a Kentucky Fried Chicken restaurant.

Multinational corporations typically modify their menus to cater to local tastes and most overseas outlets are owned by native franchisees. McDonald's in India, for example, uses lamb rather than beef in its burgers because Hinduism traditionally forbids eating beef. In Israel the majority of McDonald's restaurants are kosher and respects the Jewish shabbat, there is also a kosher McDonald's in Argentina. In Egypt and Saudi Arabia, all menu items are halal.

Additionally, multinational fast-food chains are not the only or even the primary source of fast food in most of the world. Many regional and local chains have developed around the world to compete with international chains and provide menu items that appeal to the unique regional tastes and habits. Most fast food in the developing world, however, is provided by small individual mom and pop eateries.

In Canada the majority of fast food chains are American owned, or were originally American owned but have since set up a Canadian management/headquarters location in cities such as Toronto and Vancouver. Although the case is usually American fast food chains expanding into Canada, Canadian chains such as Tim Hortons have expanded into 10 states in the United States, but are more prominent in border states such as New York and Michigan.

In the United Kingdom, many home based fast food operations were closed in the 1970s and 1980s after McDonald's became the number one outlet in the market. However, brands like Wimpy still remain, although the majority of branches became Burger King in 1989. In France and Belgium, Quick is a popular alternative to McDonald's and Burger King.

Traditional ramen and sushi restaurants still dominate fast food culture in Japan, although American outlets like Pizza Hut, McDonald's and Kentucky Fried Chicken are also popular, along with Western-style Japanese chains like Mos Burger.

In Africa, Mr. Bigg's and Tantalizers are the predominant fast food chains in Nigeria, while Nando's and Steers are predominant in South Africa.

Trends

Fast-food chains have come under fire from consumer groups (such as the Center for Science in the Public Interest, a longtime fast-food critic) over the past decade. Some of the concerns have led to the rise of the Slow Food movement. This movement seeks to preserve local cuisines and ingredients, and directly opposes laws and habits that favor fast-food choices. Among other things, it strives to educate consumers' palates to prefer what it considers richer, more varied, and more nourishing tastes of fresh local ingredients harvested in season.

Health Concerns

Some of the large fast-food chains are beginning to incorporate healthier alternatives in their menu, e.g., white meat, snack wraps, salads and fresh fruit. However, some people see these moves as a tokenistic and commercial measure, rather than an appropriate reaction to ethical concerns about the world ecology and people's health. McDonald's has announced that in March of 2006, the chain will include nutritional information on the packaging of all of its products..

Consumer Appeal

Fast-food outlets have become popular with consumers for several reasons. One is that through economies of scale in purchasing and producing food, these companies can deliver food to consumers at a very low cost. In addition, although some people dislike fast food for its predictability, it can be reassuring to a hungry person in a hurry or far from home.

In the post-war period in the United States, fast food chains like McDonald's rapidly gained a reputation for their cleanliness, fast service and a child-friendly atmosphere where families on the road could grab a quick meal, or seek a break from the routine of home cooking. Prior to the rise of the fast food chain restaurant, people generally had a choice between greasy-spoon diners where the quality of the food was often questionable and service lacking, or high-end restaurants that were expensive and impractical for families with children.

The modern, stream-lined convenience of the fast food restaurant provided a new alternative and appealed to Americans' instinct for ideas and products associated with progress, technology and innovation. Fast food restaurants rapidly became the eatery "everyone could agree on", with many featuring child-size menu combos, play areas and whimsical branding campaigns, like the iconic Ronald McDonald, designed to appeal to younger customers. Parents could have a few minutes of peace while children played or amused themselves with the toys included in their Happy Meal. There is a long history of fast food advertising campaigns, many of which are directed at children.

In other parts of the world, American and American-style fast food outlets have been popular for their quality, customer service and novelty, even though they are often the targets of popular anger towards American foreign policy or globalization more generally. Many consumers nonetheless see them as symbols of the wealth, progress and well-ordered openness of Western society and therefore become trendy attractions in many cities around the world, particularly among younger people with more varied tastes.

Innovations Timeline

- 1971: Wendy's begins drive-through service utilizing call-box technology
- 1980: 7-Eleven introduces the 32-ounce Big Gulp
- 1981: Arby's offers nutritional information
- 1994: McDonald's begins "supersizing" Extra Value Meals
- 1994: Arctic Circle becomes the first fast-food restaurant to sell Angus beef exclusively.
- 1994: Arby's is first fast-food restaurant to implement a no-smoking policy
- 2002: McDonald's cuts back on the amount of trans fat by 48 percent on french fries
- 2006: Arby's begins elimination of trans fat oils in french fries
- 2007: Starbucks announces a phase-out of trans fats on all menu items

Criticisms

Because of its convenience, fast food is popular and commercially successful in most modern societies, but it is often criticized for having the following shortcomings, among others:

- Many popular fast-food menu items are unhealthy, and excessive consumption (where excessive is generally defined as two or more times per week) can lead to obesity.

- Exploitative advertising and marketing are used, especially directed at children (which can have an adverse effect on their eating habits and health).
- It causes environmental damage through excessive packaging and clearing forests for animal rearing.
- It reduces the diversity of local cuisines.
- It survives on a low-wage, low-benefit employment model, promoting exploitative labor practices throughout the food and food service industry
- Certain franchising programs (royalties).
- Often lower quality versus sit-down restaurants.

The fast-food industry is a popular target for critics, from would-be populists like José Bové (whose destruction of a McDonald's in France made him a folk hero to some) to vegetarian activist groups such as PETA.

In his best-selling 2001 book Fast Food Nation, investigative journalist Eric Schlosser leveled a broad, socio-economic critique against the fast food industry, documenting how fast food rose from small, family-run businesses (like the hello McDonald brothers' burger joint) into large, multinational corporate juggernauts whose economies of scale radically transformed agriculture, meat processing and labor markets in the late twentieth century. While the innovations of the fast food industry gave Americans more and cheaper dining options, it has come at the price of destroying the environment, economy and small-town communities of rural America while shielding consumers from the real costs of their convenient meal, both in terms of health and the broader impact of large-scale food production and processing on workers, animals and land.

Schlosser's critics respond that fast food companies merely provide something consumers want and that the economies of scale developed by the industry have had a net positive effect on the American and global economy. Defenders of fast food companies point out that they provide entry-level jobs to people with few skills who might otherwise be unemployed and that individual consumers should be responsible for their eating choices, not business. They say that Schlosser and other critics blame fast food companies for social problems that are not of their making.

Legal Issues

In the high profile McLibel case, McDonald's took two anti-McDonald's campaigners, Helen Steel and David Morris, to court for a trial lasting two and a half years-the longest in English legal history and part of a 20-year battle-after the pair distributed leaflets critical of the company and its food in London's streets. McDonald's won the case in the UK High Court, and were awarded £60,000 damages, which later was reduced to £40,000 by the Court of Appeal. However, the court ruled in favour of a number of the defendants' claims, including that McDonald's low rates of pay depress rates across the fast-food industry. Steel and Morris then made a separate but related claim against the UK Government in the European Court of Human Rights, claiming that the lack of access to legal aid and the heavy burden of proof that lay with them to prove their claims (rather than McDonald's, the claimants, having to prove that the claims were false) under UK libel law breached the right to a fair trial and freedom of expression. The ECHR ruled against the UK Government, which subsequently introduced legislation to change the libel laws to remedy the defects highlighted by the ECHR judgment. The libel charge and fine were overturned in an appeals case.

In 2003, McDonald's was sued in a New York court by a family who claimed that the restaurant chain was responsible for their teenage daughter's obesity and attendant health problems. By manipulating food's taste, sugar and fat content and directing their advertising to children, the suit argued that the company purposely misleads the public about the nutritional value of its product. A judge dismissed the case, but the fast food industry disliked the publicity of its practices, particularly the way it targets children in its advertising. Although further lawsuits have not materialized, the issue is kept alive by in the media and political circles by those promoting the need for tort reform.

In response to this, the "Cheeseburger Bill" was passed by the U.S. House of Representatives in 2004; it later stalled in the U.S. Senate. The law was reintroduced in 2005, only to meet the same fate. This law was claimed to "[ban] frivolous lawsuits against producers and sellers of food and non-alcoholic drinks arising from obesity claims." The bill arose because of an increase in lawsuits against fast-food chains by people who claimed that eating their products made them obese, disassociating themselves from any of the blame.

SMOKE-FREE RESTAURANT

A smoke-free restaurant is a dining establishment in which smoking is banned. These restaurants are increasing in number due to the growing awareness across the world of the need to protect both employees and clients against exposure to secondhand smoke.

Relative to quitting: "One of the biggest barriers to quitting smoking is being around smoke," said the Ohio chapter's American Cancer Society Health Promotions Manager-Marianne Beard. Marianne Beard provides information on various aspects of keeping areas smokefree.

Arguments in Support

Proponents of smoke-free restaurants cite the following as benefits to barring smoking in dining establishments:

- Reduction of heart disease deaths. Medical research demonstrates that second hand tobacco smoke causes 35,000 to 40,000 excess deaths per year in the U.S. alone.

- Research suggests that the thought of more smoke-free restaurants is attracting patrons. A study in New York reports that 96 percent of those surveyed are dining out "as often" or "more often" since a smoking ban was enacted for restaurants.
- Results in a multitude of benefits for the management and safety of the restaurant, including decreasing the sick time of employees, limited liability of harm to employees and patrons, and decreased risk of fire hazards.
- Results in reduction of carbon monoxide, a contaminant present in tobacco smoke. Increased levels of carbon monoxide has been shown to cause headache, chest pain, alteration of blood pressure and nausea
- Reduction in Workers Compensation claims and fire insurance premiums.
- Reduction in synergistic adverse impacts in some locations that also have other environmental exposure health risk factors such as noise pollution and light pollution.
- More customer rotation as people do not loiter in the restaurant.

Worldwide Status

Europe used to have lesser implementation of smoke-free restaurant laws than Canada and the United States. Per capita rates of smoking are notably higher in Europe than in North America. Smoke-free restaurants have been common in the U.S. since the early 1990s, and many states have passed laws outlawing smoking in all restaurants. Some states, such as Washington, have achieved their smoking ban laws by referendum rather than by legislation. In addition to statewide bans, many large U.S. cities have banned smoking in restaurants. In 2003 New York City amended its antismoking law to include all restaurants and bars, making it one of the toughest in the U.S. The city's Department of Health found in a 2004 study that air pollution levels had decreased sixfold in bars and restaurants after the ban went into effect, and that business was largely unaffected.

Nevertheless, bans on smoking in restaurants and bars are appearing increasingly in many European countries, like Ireland (2004), Italy (2005), Sweden (2005), Norway (2004), and introduction is expected in many more in the near future. The constituent countries of the UK have enacted acts of parliament banning smoking in public places (including restaurants, bars and clubs) within Scotland by 2006, Wales and Northern Ireland by April 2007 and England by summer of 2007; significant fines of up to £2500 can be imposed upon licensees violating the ban, as well as a fifty pound fine on the smoker. In 2003 the New Zealand Parliament passed the Smokefree Environments Amendment Act which eliminates smoking in restaurants and pubs, and also places limits on smoking in other public places. In an interesting follow up study in New Zealand, restaurant patrons did not show a decline, and dining out has actually increased for non-smokers.

A more complete list of smoking bans finds hundreds of jurisdictions have enacted bans on tobacco consumption in a variety of places.

Criticism

Some restaurant owners and patrons as well as some tobacco manufacturers argue that banning tobacco smoking in restaurants deprives smokers of their access to smoking for a period of time. They also argue that restaurant patrons ought to be able to freely choose whether to enter an environment which poses health risks such as heart disease and cancer. Some patrons also suggest that smoking is an attractive adjunct to their dining experience. One British politician has stated it is unfair and inconsistent to allow prisoners to smoke and not allow the general public to smoke in restaurants.

Some others, such as libertarians say that while smoke free restaurants may have economic benefits for the restaurant that the restaurant should be free to choose for itself and should not be forced to ban smoking by the government.

Organizations

Americans for Nonsmokers' Rights and the American Nonsmokers' Rights Foundation maintain information resources and provide technical assistance and training to public health advocates and concerned citizens who would like to help achieve smokefree hospitality venues, in addition to other smokefree workplaces and enclosed public places.

7

Travel and Tourism

TRAVEL AGENCY

A travel agency is a business that sells travel related products and services, particularly package tours, to end-user customers on behalf of third party travel suppliers, such as airlines, hotels, tour companies, and cruise lines. In addition to dealing with ordinary tourists, most travel agents have a special department devoted to travel arrangements for business travellers, while some agencies specialise in commercial and business travellers. Some agencies also serve as general service agents for foreign travel companies in different countries.

ORIGINS

The British company, Cox & Kings is sometimes said to be the oldest travel agent in the world, but this rests upon services that the original bank (established in 1758) supplied to its wealthy clients. However, the modern travel agent first appeared in the second half of the nineteenth century. Thomas Cook, in addition to developing the package tour, established a chain of agencies in the last quarter of the nineteenth century, in association with the Midland Railway. These not only sold their own tours to the public, but represented other tour companies. Other British pioneer agencies were Dean and Dawson, the Polytechnic Touring Association, and the Co-operative Wholesale Society.

Travel agencies became more commonplace with the development of commercial aviation starting in the 1920s. Originally, the agencies largely catered to middle-class customers, but the post-war boom in mass-market package holidays resulted in travel agencies on the main streets of most British towns, catering to a working class clientèle looking for a cheap overseas beach holiday.

OPERATIONS

As the name implies, their main function is to act as an agent, that is to say selling travel products and services on behalf of a supplier. Consequently, unlike other retail businesses, they do not keep a stock in hand. A package holiday or a ticket is not purchased from a supplier unless a customer requests that purchase. The holiday or ticket is supplied to them at a discount. Thus, the agent's profit is the difference between the supplier's price and the price at which the product is advertised or sold to the customer. This profit is called the agency commission, and varies a great deal. In Britain, 12% would be considered a good commission.

Other commercial operations are undertaken, especially by the larger chains. These can include the sale of in-house insurance, travel guides and timetables, car rental, and the services of an on-site bureau de change dealing in the most popular holiday currencies.

The majority of travel agents have felt the need to protect themselves and their clients against the possibilities of commercial failure, either their own or a supplier. They will advertise the fact that they are bonded (posting a financial bond with an organisation). In the case of a failure, the customers are guaranteed either an equivalent holiday to that which they have lost, or (if they prefer) a refund. Many British agencies (and tour companies too) are bonded with IATA for those who issue their own tickets, ATOL for those who order tickets in, or ABTA for those who sell package holidays on behalf of a tour company.

Of course, a travel agent is supposed to offer impartial travel advice to the customer. This function almost disappeared with the mass-market package holiday, and some agency chains seemed to develop a 'holiday supermarket' concept, in which customers chose their holiday from brochures on racks and then booked it from a counter. However, a variety of social and economic changes have now contrived to bring this aspect to the fore once more, particularly the advent of multiple no-frills airlines.

TYPES OF TRAVEL AGENCY

There are three different types of agencies: these are Multiples, Miniples and Independent Agencies. The former comprise a number of national chains, often owned by international conglomerates (Thomson Holidays is now a subsidiary of TUI, the German multinational). It is now quite common for the large mass-market tour companies to purchase a controlling interest in a chain of travel agencies, in order to control the distribution of their product. (This is an example of vertical integration.)

The smaller chains are often based in particular regions or districts.

Independent Agencies usually cater for a special or niche market. Some cater to the needs of residents in an upmarket commuter town or suburb, or concentrate upon a particular area or group (catering to the travel needs of Polish expatriates, perhaps), or an activity such as sports(servicing the needs of football supporters).

CRITICISMS

Travel agencies have been accused of employing a number of restrictive practices, the chief of which is known as 'racking'. This is the practice of only displaying the brochures of those travel companies whose holidays they wish to sell, the ones that pay them the most commission. Of course, the average customer tends to think that these are the only holidays on offer, and are unaware of possible alternatives.

Generally speaking, small or specialist tour companies do not sell their product through travel agents, since they could not afford to pay the rates of commission that would be demanded. There are a few exceptions to this rule. Independent agents might sell or take bookings for local tour companies (such as coach companies) or tour companies offering specialist holidays that fit into their target market.

Consequently, even before the advent of the internet, small niche tour companies ignored travel agents and sold direct to their customers.

THE INTERNET THREAT

With the advent of general public access to the internet, many airlines and other travel companies began to sell directly to passengers. As a consequence, airlines no longer needed to pay the commissions to travel agents on each ticket sold. Since 1997, travel agencies gradually became victims of disintermediation, the reduction in costs caused by removing layers from the package holiday distribution network.

Many travel agencies have developed an internet presence by posting a website, with detailed travel information. Full travel booking sites are often complex, and require the assistance of outside travel technology solutions providers such as Travelocity, Patheo and Open Fares. These companies use travel service distribution companies who operate Global Distribution Systems (GDS), such as Sabre Holdings, Amadeus, Abaccus, Galileo and Worldspan, to provide up to the minute, detailed data on tens of thousands of flight, hotel, and car rental vacancies.

Some on-line travel sites allow visitors to compare hotel and flight rates with multiple companies for free. They often allow visitors to sort the travel packages by amenities, price, and or proximity to a city or landmark.

Travel agents have applied dynamic packaging tools to provide fully bonded (full financial protection) travel at prices equal to or lower than a member of the public can book on-line. As such, the agencies' financial assets are protected in addition to professional travel agency advice.

All travel sites that sell hotels on-line work together with numerous outside travel agents. Once the travel site sells a hotel, one of the supplying travel agents is contacted and will try to get a confirmation for this hotel. Once confirmed or not, the customer is contacted with the result. This means, that booking a hotel on a travel website will not get you an instant answer.

Only some of the hotels on a travel website can be confirmed instantly (which is normally marked as such on each site). As different travel websites work with different suppliers together, each site has different hotels that it can confirm instantly. Some examples of such on-line travel websites that sell hotel rooms are Expedia, Travelocity, Tripadvisor, Excelloz, Travel Tickets Plus and Venere.

Careers

With the many people switching to self service internet websites, the number of available jobs as travel agents is decreasing. Most jobs that become available are from older travel agents retiring. Counteracting the decrease in jobs due to internet services is the increase in the number of people travelling. Since 1995, many travel agents have exited the industry, and relatively few young people have entered the field due to less competitive salaries. However, others have abandoned the "brick and mortar" agency for a home-based business to reduce overheads, and those who remain have managed to survive by promoting other travel products such as cruise lines and train excursions, or by promoting their ability to aggressively research and assemble complex travel packages on a moment's notice (essentially acting as a very advanced concierge).

CARGO

A small number of companies work with cargo airlines and ships which are connected to cargo business.

FLIGHT ATTENDANT

In aviation flight attendants-also known as sky girls, air hostesses, stewardesses or stewards-are members of a flight crew employed by airlines to ensure the safety and comfort of the passengers aboard commercial flights.

Overview

The primary and overriding responsibility of flight attendants is passenger safety. However, they are often tasked with the secondary function of seeing to the care and comfort of the passengers, insofar as this does not interfere with their safety responsibilities. They are often perceived by the flying public as waitresses or servants because only this latter function is normally seen outside the extremely rare event of in-flight emergency; and historically this perception has been portrayed by airlines in ads and commercials.

The role of a flight attendant ultimately derives from that of similar positions on passenger ships or passenger trains, but it has more direct involvement with passengers because of the confined quarters and often shorter travel times on aircraft. Additionally, the job of a flight attendant revolves around safety to a much greater extent than those of similar staff on other forms of transportation. Flight attendants on board a flight collectively form a cabin crew, as distinguished from pilots and engineers on the flight deck.

Outside the exceptional case of an in-flight emergency, flight attendants usually provide courtesy services for passengers, such as preparation distribution of in-flight meals and drinks, management of in-flight entertainment systems, sale of duty-free and other merchandise, and the like. As the most visible representatives of their airlines, their importance to customer relations and the image of their airlines is considerable. Many jurisdictions mandate the presence of flight attendants on commercial aircraft, based on the passenger capacity of the aircraft and other factors. This mandate generally relates only to their function as safety technicians.

Qualifications

Training

Flight attendants are normally trained in the hub or headquarters city of an airline over a period that may run from six weeks to six months, depending on the country. The main focus of training is safety. One flight attendant is required for every 50 passenger seats on board in the United States, but many airlines have chosen to increase that number. One of the most elaborate training facilities was Breech Academy which TWA opened in 1969 in Overland Park, Kansas, United States. Other airlines were to also send their attendants to the school. However, during the fare wars the school's viability declined and it closed around 1990.Safety training includes, but is not limited to: emergency passenger evacuation management, use of evacuation slides / life rafts, in-flight fire fighting, survival in the jungle / sea / desert / ice, first aid, CPR, defibrillation, ditching / emergency landing procedures, decompression emergencies, crew resource management and security.

Language

Multilingual flight attendants are often in demand to accommodate international travellers. The languages most in demand, other than English, are Mandarin, Cantonese, Japanese, French, German, Spanish, and Portugese.

Height and Weight

Some airlines, such as EVA Air, have height requirements for purely aesthetic purposes. Horizon Air and other regional carriers have height restrictions because their aircraft have low ceilings. A typical acceptable range is from 5'2" (1.57 m) to 6'0" (1.83 m). Flight attendants are also subject to weight requirements as well. Weight must usually be in proportion to height; persons outside the normal range may not be qualified to act as flight attendants.

History

The first flight attendant, a steward, was reportedly a man on the German Zeppelin LZ10 Schwaben in 1911. Imperial Airways of the United Kingdom had "cabin boys" or "stewards" in the 1920s. In the USA, Stout Airways was the first to employ stewards in 1926, working on Ford Tri-Motor planes between Detroit and Grand Rapids, Michigan. Western Air Express (1928) and Pan Am (1929) were the first US carriers to employ stewards to serve food. Ten-passenger Fokker Aircraft used in the Caribbean had stewards in the era of gambling trips to Havana, Cuba from Key West, Florida. The first female flight attendant was a 25-year-old registered nurse named Ellen Church: Hired by United Airlines in 1930, she also first envisioned nurses on aircraft.

Other airlines followed suit, hiring nurses to serve as stewardesses on most of their flights. The requirement to be a registered nurse was relaxed at the start of World War II, as so many nurses enlisted into the armed forces.

Uniforms

The first stewardess uniforms were designed to be durable, practical, and inspire confidence in passengers. The first stewardesses for United Airlines wore green berets, green capes and nurse's shoes. Other airlines, such as Eastern Airlines, actually dressed stewardesses in nurses' uniforms.

Perhaps reflecting the military aviation background of many commercial aviation pioneers, many early uniforms had a strongly military appearance; hats, jackets, and skirts showed simple straight lines and military details like epaulets and brass buttons. Many uniforms had a summer and winter version, differentiated by colours and fabrics appropriate to the season: navy blue for winter, for example, khaki for summer. But as the role of women in the air grew, and airline companies began to realize the publicity value of their stewardesses, more feminine lines and colours began to appear in the late 1930s and early 1940s. Some airlines began to commission designs from high-end department stores and still others called in noted designers or even milliners to create distinctive and attractive apparel.

Unions

Flight attendant unions were formed, beginning at United Airlines in the 1940s, to negotiate improvements in pay, benefits and working conditions. Those unions would later challenge what they perceived as sexist stereotypes and unfair work practices such as age limits, size limits, limitations on marriage, and prohibition of pregnancy. Many of these limitations have been lifted by judicial mandates. The largest flight attendants union is the Association of Flight Attendants, representing over 50,000 flight attendants at 22 airlines within the United States.

In the United Kingdom, cabin crew can be represented by either Cabin Crew '89, or the much larger and more powerful Transport and General Workers Union.

Discrimination

Airline managers commonly subjected flight attendants to various forms of discrimination from the early days of the profession until the 1990s. Flight attendants at US-based airlines, and others as well, were forced to resign or were fired if they got married, if they were overweight, wore eyeglasses, if they turned 30 years of age (or 32 at some airlines). These discriminatory policies came under attack in the United States after passage of Title VII of the Civil

Rights Act of 1964. Flight attendant unions like the Association of Flight Attendants used Title VII, in the courts and at the bargaining table, to bring an end to such practices and recognize the professionalism of the flight attendant career.

The no-marriage rule was eliminated throughout the US airline industry by the 1980s. The last such broad categorical discrimination, the weight restrictions, were eliminated in the 1990s through litigation and negotiations. By the end of the 1970s, the term stewardess had generally been replaced by the gender-neutral, and more wordy, alternative flight attendant. More recently the term cabin crew has begun to replace 'flight attendants,' because of the term's recognition of their role as members of the crew.

September 11, 2001

The role of flight attendants received heightened prominence after the September 11, 2001 attacks when flight attendants (such as Sandra W. Bradshaw, Robert Fangman, CeeCee Lyles, Renee May, Betty Ong and Madeline Amy Sweeney) actively attempted to protect passengers from assault, and also provided vital information to air traffic controllers on the hijackings.

In the wake of the terror attacks of September 11, 2001, many flight attendants at major airlines were laid off on account of decreased passenger loads.

Roles in an Emergency

Actions of flight attendants in emergencies have long been credited in saving lives; in the United States, the NTSB and other aviation authorities view flight attendants as essential for safety, and are thus required on Part 121 aircraft operations. Studies, some done in light of the Manchester air disaster, have concluded that assertive cabin crew are essential for the rapid evacuation of airplanes. Notable examples of cabin crew actions include:

- Scandinavian Airlines Flight 751, when cabin crew recognized an emergency landing was imminent and commanded the passengers to "bend down...hold your knees" to adopt the brace position.
- A Delta Connection (Atlantic Southeast Airlines) flight attendant who provided emergency briefings, brace and evacuation commands to the passengers when a EMB-120 Brasilia aircraft sustained serious damage to one of its engine and crash landed. She was the only flight attendant on board. The NTSB acccident report commended "the exemplary manner in which the flight attendant briefed the passengers and handled the emergency".
- British Airways Flight 5390, in which a flight attendant was able to prevent a pilot from being lost through a cockpit window that had failed.
- Southern Airways Flight 242, on which the cabin crew provided safety briefings to their passengers, and on their own initiative, warned passengers of the impending crash by commanding passengers to adopt the brace position. At least one flight attendant is known to have assisted in rescuing trapped passengers.
- Air Florida Flight 90, in which the lone surviving flight attendant passed the only lifevest she could find to another passenger. She is recognized in the NTSB report for this "unselfish act."
- TWA flight attendant Uli Derickson who protected passengers during the TWA Flight 847 hijacking by assisting with negotiation efforts.
- TWA Flight 843, when a TWA L-1011 aircraft crashed after an aborted takeoff in 1992. The aircraft was destroyed by fire. Nine flight attendants, along with five off-duty flight attendants, evacuated all 292

persons on board without loss of life. The NTSB in their after accident reported noted, "The performance of the flight attendants during the emergency was exceptional and probably contributed to the success of the emergency evacuation."

- On British Airways Flight 2069, cabin crew stopped the plane from being crashed by a mentally ill passenger. It was a highly mediatized episode of air rage.
- Crew on American Airlines Flight 63 prevented a shoe bomber from blowing up the plane.
- Flight attendants on Qantas flight 1737 prevented their plane from being hijacked by a passenger with mental health issues. Two of them were taken to hospital with stab wounds.
- Aloha Airlines Flight 243 suffered a decompression which tore an 18-foot section of fuselage away from the plane. Despite her injuries, flight attendant Michelle Honda crawled up and down the aisle reassuring passengers.
- Senior Purser Neerja Bhanot saved the lives of passengers and crew when Pan Am Flight 73 was hijacked. She was killed while protecting children from the terrorists. After her death she received the Special Courage Award from the United States Department of Justice.
- Flight Attendants on Air Canada Flight 797 used procedures which were not specifically taught in training such as instruction passengers to open over wing window exits to allow passengers to evacuate quicker, moving passengers to the front of the aircraft to move them away from the fire and smoke, and passing out towels for passengers to cover their nose and mouths with while the cabin was filling with smoke.

8

The Travel Technology

INTRODUCTION

Travel technology is a term used to describe applications of Information Technology (IT), or Information and Communications Technology (ICT), in travel, tourism and hospitality industry. Travel technology may also be referred to as tourism technology or even hospitality automation. Web 2.0 is a current buzzword in the travel technology community, used to describe various social software applications. XML is an increasingly important aspect of travel technology for handling metadata toward the semantic web. Immigration technology, known as tecurity, such as the biometric passport may also be included as travel technology in the broad sense.

DEFINITION

Since travel implies locomotion, travel technology was originally associated with the computer reservations system (CRS) of the airlines industry, but now is used more inclusively, incorporating the broader tourism sector as well as its subset the hospitality industry. While travel technology includes the computer reservations system, it also represents a much broader range of applications, in fact increasingly so. Travel technology may also be referred to as e-travel / etravel or e-tourism / etourism (eTourism), in reference to "electronic travel" or "electronic tourism".

In other contexts, the term "travel technology" can refer to technology intended for use by travellers, such as lightweight laptop computers with universal power supplies or satellite Internet connections. That is not the sense in which it is used here.

THE APPLICATIONS

Travel technology includes many processes such as dynamic packaging which provide useful new options for consumers. Today the tour guide can be a GPS tour guide, and the guidebook could be an audioguide, podguide or I-Tours, such as City audio guides.

HISTORY

Certainly travel technology was born on the coattails of the airline industry's use of automation and their need to extend this out to the travel agency partners. It should be kept in mind that there was an on-line world before the advent of the world wide web in the form of private and commercial on-line services, via packet switched network using X.25. Travel technology played a significant role in the so-called dot-com boom and bust, circa 1997-2001.

IN-FLIGHT ENTERTAINMENT

In-flight entertainment (IFE) refers to the entertainment available to aircraft passengers during a flight. After World War II commercial aviation flights became a daily event in which entertainment was requested by passengers to help the time pass. This was delivered in the form of food and drink services, along with an occasional projector movie during lengthy flights. The concept of IFE took on a new meaning starting in the 1980s. In 1985 the first personal audio player was offered to passengers, along with noise cancelling headphones in 1989. During the 1990s the demand for better IFE was a major factor in the way airlines designed and retrofitted their cabins. Before then, the most a passenger could expect was a movie projected on a screen at the front of a cabin, which could be heard via a headphone socket at their seat.

Major manufacturers of IFE systems include Panasonic Avionics Corporation, Thales Group, Honeywell Rockwell Collins and LiveTV. Most of the difficulties these producers encounter are traditional to those of avionic electronic systems. Such issues are system safety, cost efficiency, software reliability, hardware maintenance, and user compatibility.

History

The first in-flight entertainment began to first appear in the 1960s on Boeing 707 and Douglas DC-8 aircraft. These early in-flight entertainment systems consisted of in-seat audio that can be heard with hollow tube headphones. When widebody aircraft (such as the Boeing 747 and McDonnell Douglas DC-10) began to enter service, the first video systems began to appear, featuring a film projected onto a screen. In the late 1970s and early 1980s, CRT-based projectors began to appear on newer widebody aircraft, such as the Boeing 767. Some airlines upgraded the old film IFE systems to the CRT-based systems in the late 1980s and early 1990s on some of their older widebodies. Around the same time, CRT-based displays began to appear over the aisles of narrowbody and widebody aircraft. In the mid 1990s, the first in-seat video systems began to appear, and LCD technology started to replace CRT technology as the display technology of choice for overhead video. In the late 1990s and early 2000s, the first in-seat audio/video on-demand systems began to appear.

IFE is offered as an option on almost all wide body aircraft in service today, while some narrow body aircraft are not equipped with any form of IFE at all. This is mainly due to the aircraft storage and weight limits. The Boeing 757 was the first narrow body aircraft to widely feature both audio and video IFE and today it is rare to find a 757 without an IFE system. Most 757s feature ceiling-mounted CRT screens, although some newer 757s may feature drop-down LCDs. Many Airbus A320 series and Boeing 737NG aircraft are also equipped with drop-down LCD screens. Some airlines, such as WestJet and Delta Air Lines, have equipped some narrow body aircraft with personal video screens at every seat. Others, such as Air Canada, have even equipped some regional jets with audio-video on demand (AVOD).

System Safety and Regulation

One major obstacle of creating an IFE system is the system's safety. With the sometimes miles of wiring involved, voltage leaks and arcing become a problem. To contain any possible issues, the IFE system is typically isolated from the aircraft's main systems. In the US, in order for a company's product to be considered safe and reliable, it must be certified by the FAA and pass all of the applicable requirements found in the Federal Aviation Regulations. The concerning section, or title, dealing with the aviation industry and the electronic systems embedded in the aircraft, is CFR title 14 part 25. Contained inside part 25 are many specific rules, each relating to a specific portion of the aircraft's electronic system. There are two major codes that regulate IFE systems and their safety: code 1301 which approves the electronic equipment for installation and use, by assuring that the system in question is properly labeled, and that its design is appropriate to its intended function. Code 1309 states that the electrical equipment must not alter the safety or functionality of the aircraft upon the result of a failure. In order for the intended IFE system to pass this code, it must be independent from that of the aircraft's main power source and processor. By separating the power supplies and data links from that of the aircraft's performance processor, in the event of a failure the system is self sustained, and can not alter the functionality of the aircraft. Upon the completion of all applicable codes the IFE system is up to standards for use in the United States, however the rules and regulations may be different when applying for use in other countries.

Cost Efficiency

Further complicating issues when creating a safe IFE system is the concept of cost efficiency. The large companies currently involved, along with those future prospects, are in a constant battle to cut costs of production, without cutting the systems quality and compatibility. Cutting production cost consists of anything from altering the housing for personal televisions, to reducing the amount of embedded software in the IFE processor. Difficulties with cost are also present with the customers, or airlines, looking to purchase IFE systems. Most IFE systems are purchased by existing airlines as an upgrade package to an existing fleet of aircraft. This cost can be anywhere from $2 Million-$5 Million for seat back LCD monitors, with an embedded IFE system. Some of the IFE systems are being purchased already installed in a new aircraft, such as the Airbus A320, which eliminates the possibility of having upgrade difficulties. Each airline is finding interesting ways to pass on this additional cost to their customers. Some airlines are passing the cost directly into the customers ticket price, while some are charging a user fee based on an individual customers use. Some are also attempting to get a majority of the cost paid for by advertisements on, around, and in their IFE.

Software Reliability

Software for IFE systems must be aesthetically pleasing, dependent, reliable, compatible, and also must be user friendly. These restrictions account for expensive engineering of individually specific software. In addition to the regular software reliability issues, comes the issue of the software being touch screen sensitive, allowing interaction between each seat in the aircraft and the flight attendants, which is wireless in some systems. Along with a complete aircraft intranet to deal with, the software of the IFE system must be reliable when communicating to and from the main IFE processor. These additional requirements not only place an additional strain on the software engineers, but also on the price. Boundary value errors can slip through the testing phases of the software and, once installed, truly cause problems.

Varieties of in-flight Entertainment

Cabin Music

Soft music is often piped through the PA system and is heard in the cabin upon boarding, disembarkation, taxiing and take-off of the aircraft. The music is often chosen to be pleasant and soothing, and exhibits characteristics similar to elevator music. In accord with the cabin music, some airlines are now installing music in the restrooms. This is done to ease some of those who become sick and uncomfortable while in the air.

Cabin Lighting

A recent addition to commercial aircraft with IFE systems, cabin lighting allows the IFE system to adjust the cabins LED overhead lighting system when appropriate. Implemented through software, the lighting in the cabin can be adjusted through an array of colors, from a deep purple to a refreshing neon green. The lighting is also beginning to be implemented as to follow the cabin music currently playing. The first major implementation of cabin lighting is present in the new Virgin America Airbus A-320's.

Audio Entertainment

Audio entertainment is provided in the form of several selected channels a passenger may choose covering various genres of music, as well as news, information and comedy. Much like radio shows, most music channels are pre-recorded and feature their own DJs to provide chatter, song introductions and interviews with featured artists.

In audio-video on demand (AVOD) systems, software such as MusicMatch is used to select music off the music server. Phillips Music Server is one of the most widely used servers running under Windows Media Center used to control AVOD systems.

This form of in-flight entertainment is experienced through headphones that are distributed to the passengers after take-off.

The headphone plugs are usually only compatible with the audio socket on the passenger's armrest (and vice-versa), and some airlines may charge a small fee in order to obtain a pair. The headphones provided can also be used for the viewing of personal televisions, if any.

Recent IFE systems have been made compatible with XM Satellite Radio, and also with I-Pod's, allowing for passengers to access their own accounts, or bring their own music, along with offering extensive libraries of full audio CD's from an assortment of artists.

Video Entertainment

Traditionally, video entertainment is provided via a large video screen at the front of a cabin section, as well as smaller monitors situated every few rows above the aisles. Sound is supplied via the same headphones distributed for audio entertainment.

However in recent times, personal televisions (PTVs) for every passenger have become more popular, providing passengers with a selection of channels broadcasting new and classic films, as well as comedies, documentaries, children's shows and drama series.

Some airlines also present news and current affairs programming, which are often pre-recorded and delivered in the early morning before flights commence.

PTVs are operated via an In flight Management System which stores pre-recorded channels on a central server, and streams them to PTV equipped seats during flight. AVOD systems store individual programs separately, allowing a passenger to have a specific program streamed to them privately, and be able to control the playback. Some airlines also provide video games as part of the video entertainment system.

For example, Singapore Airlines passengers have access to a number of Super Nintendo games as part of its KrisWorld entertainment system. Also Virgin America's new RED Entertainment System offers passengers a wide variety of internet gaming over a Linux-based operating system. RED also provides an open source gaming link, so passengers who are experienced in writing games can upload certain created games to the server.

In-flight Movies

The first motion picture to be played on an airline, was a silent film shown on a Deutsch Lufthansa flight over Germany in 1925. Regularly scheduled in flight movies began to premiere in 1961 on flights from New York to Los Angeles.Today there are various types of in flight movies that are offered.

There are those personal on demand videos which are stored in an aircraft main IFE computer system. From there they can be viewed on demand by the user as they choose. Along with the on demand concept comes the ability for the user to pause, rewind, fast forward, or jump to any point in the movie. There are also the movies that are commonly shown throughout the aircraft at one time usually on a screen in the front of the cabin.

Personal Televisions

Most major airlines have now installed personal televisions (otherwise known as PTVs) for every passenger on most long-haul routes. These televisions are usually located in the seat-backs or tucked away in the armrests for front row seats and first class. Many different systems are used and vary from different airlines.

There are those that utilize a few channels, or direct broadcast satellite television which enable passengers to view live TV broadcasts. Some airlines also offer video games using PTV equipment.

In accordance with increasing amenities being provided on board flights, audio-video on demand (AVOD) entertainment has also been introduced. This enables passengers to pause, rewind, fast-forward or stop a program that they have been watching.

This is in contrast to older entertainment systems where no interactivity is provided for. AVOD also allows the passengers to choose between an assortment of movies stored in the aircraft computer system.

With the introduction of new aircraft and the rapid advances in aviation technology, it is rare to find new long-haul planes being delivered without PTVs. Lufthansa is the only airline in the world to order new long haul aircraft like the Boeing 747 without fitting PTVs in Economy Class.

Moving-map Systems

A moving-map system is a real-time flight information video channel broadcast through PTVs and cabin video screens. In addition to displaying a map that illustrates the current position and direction of the plane, the system also reveals details concerning the flight to passengers such as the altitude, airspeed, distance to destination, distance from origination and local time.

Moving-map system information is derived from the aircraft's flight computer systems. It is often generically referred to as Airshow, one of the first moving-map systems now owned by Rockwell Collins. Panasonic Avionics Corporation now offers a similar product known as iXPLOR on their latest IFE systems. Honeywell also offers a similar product known as JetMap.

Data Communication

IFE producers have begun to introduce intranet type systems into their designs. Virgin America's RED Entertainment System allows for passengers to chat amongst one another, compete against each other in the provided games, talk to the flight attendants and request, and pay for in advance, food or drinks, and have full access to the internet and email.

In an upcoming Airbus A380 aircraft, data communication via satellite system will allow passengers to connect to live Internet from the individual IFE units or their laptops via the in-flight Wi-Fi access..

Next-generation Systems

Currently there are only a few complete IFE systems incorporating live data/TV and on-demand capabilities. Jet Blue's personal television with limited audio and video files on demand, including XM radio and DirectTV is an example of one of the more advanced IFE systems deployed today. Air Canada also provides their passengers with PTV's accompanied by a pre-arranged selection of movies and video games that are rescheduled monthly.

Currently there are three IFE Systems in the aviation industry that are billed as "next-generation", Singapore Airlines' KrisWorld, Emirates Airlines' ICE Entertainment, and the soon-to-be-released RED entertainment system from Virgin America.

KrisWorld

Audio, Video, and Games on Demand

Installed in Singapore Airlines' new Boeing 777-300ER aircraft, KrisWorld is an example of a next-generation IFE

System. Currently boasting the highest resolution of any IFE at 1280 x 768 pixels, these personal LCD displays are located in the seat back in front of the passenger.

KriWorld contains 80 on-demand movies for passenger viewing, a predetermined assortment of television shows, 12 music channels and 180 CD titles on demand. KrisWorld has also contracted with Nintendo to provide 91 Nintendo game titles for passenger use on demand.

KrisWorld Interactive

KrisWorld also includes Flight Path, an improvement on the existing moving map system present in most IFEs. KrisWorld also includes a feature dubbed Destination Info, an interactive guidebook for each of Singapore Airlines destination cities. Destination Info gives passengers access to street directions, restaurant guides, and local event listings for a particular day.

Live Text News is KrisWorld's in-flight news service. It updates via satellite once every hour, and includes content on the stock market, local news,sports, and weather.

Language Tutorials

KrisWorld is also the first IFE system to introduce Berlitz World Traveler as a feature of their IFE. Berlitz World Traveler is a program that assists passengers in learning any one of 22, providing access to tutorials and quizzes.

ICE

Information

Operated by Emirates Airline, ICE is another example of a next-generation in-flight entertainment system. ICE (Information Communication Entertainment) is currently operating in all of Emirates Airline's Airbus A340-500, and all of Emirates Airline's Boeing 777-300ER and Boeing 777-200 fleet.

ICE provides passengers with a direct data link to BBC News. ICE is the first IFE system to be connected directly to automatic news updates.

This is complemented by ICE's Airshow moving-map software from Rockwell Collins. Along with this software comes ICE's unique system of exterior cameras located on the aircraft. These cameras can be viewed by any passenger through the IFE system during takeoff and landing.

Communication

ICE also contains a link to an in-flight email server which allows passengers to access, send or receive emails for US $1 per message. Similar to KrisWorld, ICE also contains a seat-to-seat chat server.

Entertainment

Similar to KrisWorld, the entertainment system from Singapore Airlines, ICE allows passengers to choose from a library of movies, audio CDs, and video games. ICE offers over 130 on-demand movie titles and 15 video-on-demand channels, 60 prerecorded television channels, 350 audio channels, and around 50 video-game titles. ICE can also be accessed in 10 different languages are English, French, Spanish, Arabic, Korean, and Japanese.

Virgin America's RED

Audio, Video, and Gaming

Set to premiere in summer of 2007, Virgin America's RED IFE system will be installed in all of Virgin America's Airbus A320's. RED allows similar functions to KrisWorld's and ICE's IFE system.

RED allows passengers to watch live TV, including 18 live TV channels provided by Dish Network. RED also provides 25 on-demand pay-per-view movies, over 2000 MP3 audio tracks, and more than 20 audio channels. Access is provided through a 9", 1024x768-pixel LCD touch screen monitor located in the seat back in front of each passenger. One of RED's unique characteristics is passengers' ability to create play lists of movies and MP3s. RED is built upon a Linux platform, and Virgin America plans to use Linux' open source nature to port games for in-flight use.

RED Interactive

RED's controller is the first to provide a QWERTY keyboard. Another interactive feature of RED is the ability passengers have to bring along their own keyboard, or mouse and use the provided USB port to use their own devices with the IFE system. Passengers can also directly order food and drinks from the flight attendants from the menu section of the IFE. All paid-for services such as movies and food can be paid for by the credit card reader located at the bottom of the IFE screen. RED also offers passengers full broadband access to chat, and instant message amongst passengers, along with having unrestricted access to the internet, and email.

9

A MOTEL

INTRODUCTION

Entering dictionaries after World War II, the word motel (portmanteau of "motor and hotel" or "motorists' hotel") referred initially to a single building of connected rooms whose doors face a parking lot and/or common area or a series of small cabins with common parking. Their creation was driven by increased driving distances on the United States highway system that allowed easy cross-country travel.

HISTORY

The concept originated with the Motel Inn of San Luis Obispo, constructed in 1925 by Arthur Heineman. This word was not invented by Mr. James Peat.

Unlike their predecessors, auto camps and tourist courts, motels quickly adopted a homogenized appearance. Typically one would find an 'I' or 'L' or 'U' shaped structure that included rooms, an attached manager's office, a reception which usually takes up the space of one guest room and perhaps a small diner.

Postwar motels sought more visual distinction, often featuring eye-catching neon signs which employed pop culture themes that ranged from Western imagery of cowboys and Indians to contemporary images of spaceships and atomic symbols.

The motel began in the 1920s as mom-and-pop motor courts on the outskirts of a town. They attracted the first road warriors as they crossed the United States in their new automobiles. They usually had a grouping of small cabins and their anonymity made them ideal trysting places (or the "hot trade" in industry lingo).

Even the famous outlaws Bonnie and Clyde were frequent guests, using motels as hideouts. The motels' potential for breeding perceived lust and larceny alarmed then FBI chief J. Edgar Hoover, who attacked motels and auto camps in an article he penned called "Camps of Crime", which ran in the February 1940 issue of American Magazine.

Motels differed from hotels in their emphasis on largely anonymous interactions between owners and occupants, their location along highways (as opposed to urban cores), and their orientation to the outside (in contrast to hotels whose doors typically face an interior hallway). Motels almost by definition included a parking lot, while older hotels were not built with automobile parking in mind.

With the 1952 introduction of Kemmons Wilson's Holiday Inn, the 'mom and pop' motels of that era went into decline. Eventually, the emergence of the interstate highway system, along with other factors, led to a blurring of the motel and the hotel.

Today, family owned motels with as few as five rooms may still be found along older highways. The quality and standards of every independent motel differ, so it is always wise to cruise around for a good motel before settling in a room.

LONG-STAY ACCOMMODATION

Motels with low rates sometimes serve as housing for people who are not able to afford an apartment or have recently lost their home and need somewhere to stay until further arrangements are made.

SHORT-TIME

In most countries of Latın America and some countries of East Asia, motels are also known as short-time hotels, and offer a short-time or "transit" stay with hourly rates primarily intended for people having sexual liaisons and not requiring a full nights accommodation.

In Mexico love hotel equivalents are known as "Motel de paso" (Passing Motel) (even if they are actually meant mostly for pedestrian access). In Argentina these establishments are called albergue transitorio ("temporary lodging"), though known as telo in vesre-slang.

In Singapore, cheap hotels often offer a slightly more euphemistic "transit" stay for short-time visitors. In Manila, a campaign against the hotels, believed by religious conservatives to contribute to social decay in the predominantly Roman Catholic country, ended with the city banning hotels from offering stays of very short duration. As of December 2006 there are still many short time hotels in operation. In Belgium and France, these establishments are known as hotels de passe. In Chile, they are known as moteles parejeros (coupling motels), and many of them offer hourly rates. In the United States and Canada, some ordinary motels in low income areas-often called no-tell motels-play a similar role to love hotels.

LOVE HOTEL

A love hotel (rabu hoteru) is a type of short-stay hotel found in Japan operated primarily for the purpose of allowing couples privacy to have sex.

Love hotels usually offer a room rate for a "rest", kyukei as well as an overnight night stay. The period of a "rest" varies, typically ranging from one to three hours. Cheaper daytime off-peak rates are common. In general, reservations are not possible, leaving the hotel will forfeit access to the room, and overnight stay rates only become available after 10pm.

They are often used by young couples, since many young Japanese people live with their parents. They are also commonly used for prostitution.

Entrances are discreet and interaction with staff is minimized, with rooms often selected from a panel of buttons and the bill settled by pneumatic tube, automatic cash machines, or a pair of hands behind a pane of frosted glass. While cheaper hotels are utilitarian, higher-end hotels may feature fanciful rooms decorated with cartoon characters, equipped with rotating beds, ceiling mirrors, karaoke machines or decked out like dungeons complete with S&M gear.

These hotels are typically either concentrated in certain city districts such as Dogenzaka in Shibuya, Tokyo, near highways on the city outskirts, or in industrial districts. Few Japanese people wish to have a love hotel in their neighbourhood, and construction in residential areas is often opposed.

Love hotel architecture is sometimes garish, with buildings shaped like castles, boats or UFOs and lit with lurid pink and purple neon lighting. However, many love hotels are very ordinary looking buildings, distinguished mainly by having small or covered windows.

In recent years, the love hotel business has drawn the interest of the structured finance industry. Several transactions have been completed where the cash flows from a number of hotels have been securitised and sold to international investors and buy-out funds.

History

In Japan, love hotels developed from tea rooms chaya, mostly used by prostitutes and their clients, but also by lovers. After World War II, the name tsurekomi yado, literally "bring-along inn" was adopted, originally for simple lodgings run by families with a few rooms to spare. These establishments appeared first around Ueno, Tokyo in part due to demand from Occupation forces, and boomed after 1958 when legal prostitution was abolished and the trade moved underground. The introduction of the automobile in the 1960s brought with it the "motel" and further spread the concept.

The name "love hotel" may originate from an establishment in Osaka called Hotel Love, which had a revolving advertisement on the roof, with "Love" on one side, and "Hotel" on the other. The sign was thus easy to misread as "love hotel", which was adopted for the entire concept. The original term has since fallen into disuse thanks to the euphemism treadmill and an ever-changing palette of terms is used by hotel operators keen on representing themselves as more fashionable than the competition. Alternative names include romance hotel, fashion hotel, leisure hotel, amusement hotel, couples hotel and boutique hotel.

10

Revenue Management for the Hospitality Industry

INTRODUCTION

When you stayed in that luxury hotel during your last vacation, did you check what your neighbor paid for her room? If she were a business visitor, she could have paid well above $300 for the same room that you paid $180. It is also possible that she paid $120 provided she planned well in advance and managed to get that "better" deal which was elusive to you. So why do hotels charge different customers different rates for the same type of room?

Such differences are the result of an increasingly common strategy to maximize revenue (and profits) in the Hotel industry--a practice referred to as Revenue or Yield Management.

Revenue Management (RM) is a scientific technique that combines Operations Research, Statistics and Customer Relationship Management (CRM) and categorizes customers into price bands, based on various services. Statistical analysis of past data helps in forecasting demand and establishing the appropriate price bands. Applied correctly, Revenue Management helps hotels expand market size and increase revenues. Some industry practitioners also refer to RM as the art of selling the right room to the right customer at the right time and for the right price.

To understand the need for an RM system, let us take the following two examples. At the peak of the SARS epidemic in Canada, a resort experienced a 25% drop in number of visitors. Amazingly, this resort managed to limit decline in revenue to a bare 3%. During economic depression, a travel management company reduced its marketing budget by half, but still managed a revenue increase of 6%. How were these successes possible? The answer to both of these questions lies with the implementation of Revenue Management strategy.

WHY REVENUE MANAGEMENT?

- Segmented Market: Hotels typically segment their market (customer base) into a set of categories based on the price each category is willing to pay. Typical categories include the business traveler and the vacation traveler. Because demand patterns for each of these categories may vary significantly, hotels find it difficult to satisfy all of the demand simultaneously. A good example is the comparison between the time-conscious business executive and the pricesensitive vacation customer. The former is willing to pay a higher price in exchange for flexibility of being able to book a room at the last minute while the latter is willing to give up some flexibility for the sake of a more inexpensive room. RM tries to maximize revenues by managing the tradeoff between a low occupancy and higher room rate scenario (business customers) versus a high occupancy and lower room rate (vacation customers). Such a strategy allows hotels to fill rooms that would otherwise have been empty.
- *Fixed Capacity*: A hotel's capacity is relatively fixed-it is nearly impossible to add or remove rooms based on fluctuations in demand. If at all hotel capacity were flexible, there would be no need to manage capacity.

- *Perishable Inventory*: In the hotel industry, hotel rooms are the inventory. A hotel room that remains unoccupied for a night loses all its value for that night. This inventory cannot be stored and is lost forever. Because RM tries to manage demand instead of supply, it proves to be good business sense for the hotel.
- *Low Marginal Cost*: The fixed cost of adding a room in a hotel is heavily capital intensive. However, once the hotel manages to cover its initial fixed costs, the cost of serving an additional customer is low enough that the hotel can sell the room at a lower margin if it wishes. Such a strategy will obviously need to be balanced by one that also seeks to sell the room(s) at higher margins. Thus, the high fixed cost/low marginal cost nature of the business makes price differentiation a necessity-something that is made possible by application of RM.
- *Advanced Sales*: More often than not, requests for bookings start early. Therefore, hotels have enough leeway to adjust room prices based on the variation between realized bookings and expected demand. If all hotel rooms are sold at the same time, the hotel does not have the flexibility to adjust prices upward if demand picks up later. The tradeoff occurs when a manager is faced with the option of accepting an early reservation from a customer who wants a low price, or waiting to see if a higher paying customer will eventually show up...
- *Demand Fluctuations*: Demand for hotel rooms is characterized by crests and troughs, which the hotel factors in during the room pricing process. In peak season, the hotel can increase its revenues by raising room prices, while during lean seasons it can increase its utilization rate by lowering prices. Past data will offer the manager a way to forecast when these periods

of high and low demand may occur. Unfortunately, it is very difficult to predict the actual demand with a high degree of certainty.

Therefore, the most critical challenge facing the hotel industry is predicting potential capacity, and developing a pricing strategy that will encourage maximum capacity and revenue. Revenue Management is the most effective technique to solve this challenge, similar to aggregate and hierarchical production planning techniques often employed in the manufacturing industry.

Revenue Management is based on complex optimization methodologies developed from advanced statistical and analytical models. In order to arrive at a solution, managers need to evaluate several millions of decisions, which requires a significant investment of skills, hardware and time. Many RM practitioners prefer to breakdown the actual business scenario into four sub-problems, and then identify an individual solution to some or all of these sub-problems. This would significantly reduce the number of potential non-optimal decisions thereby providing fewer choices, leading to quicker results.

These four sub-problems are:

(a) Market segment identification,

(b) Forecasting and Pricing,

(c) Inventory allocation, and

(d) Overbooking.

How does it all Work?

Market Segment Identification: The first and foremost step in a hotel RM system is the identification of the various market segments for the hotel room, followed by implementation of a differential pricing scheme. The objective in front of the hotel is the expansion of its market and in motivating the customer to pay more than he/she will usually spend. It is further observed that customers in the business class segment are less sensitive to higher prices as opposed to those in the vacation segment. An RM system helps hotels create additional price-points by building physical and logical fences around the different market segments, as shown in the table below.

CHARACTERISTICS	HIGHER PRICE	LOWER PRICE
Physical Fences		
View	Pool view, ocean view, hill view	Non-scenic view
Size	Bigger room with more facilities and gadgets	Smaller rooms with fewer facilities
Temporal	Weekday bookings	Weekend bookings
Logical Fences		
Length of Stay	Short stay. Often one or two days	Longer stay. One night revenue can spoil three nights revenue when demand is high
Flexibility	Cancellations and rescheduling are allowed at a low penalty	High penalty for cancellation and schedule changes
Time of Purchase	Bookings are made very close to date of check-in	Bookings are made quite early
Privileges	Are rewarded loyalty privileges either as free services or free stay vouchers	No privileges
Size of Business Provided	Corporate business customers booking frequently	Self funding vacationers booking rarely
Point of Sale	Physical delivery and confirmations	By email or phone

Demand Forecasting: The next step in an RM process is forecasting demand and pricing of the different market segments. Pricing and demand are inter-related and need to be coordinated. In the hotel industry, demand for a room is cyclic in nature (day of a week, months of a year) and follows a trend (demand growth due to economic growth). These forecasts are seldom precise but provide the decision-maker with an approximate set of inputs that are used in the planning process. RM models help pinpoint demand by minimizing uncertainty and producing the best possible forecast.

Allocation: The next important step in a RM process is the allocation of inventory (hotel rooms) among different market segments. The ratio of discounted versus full priced rooms is not fixed during the reservation period; rather, it is "tweaked" appropriately as the date of stay approaches. The opportunity cost of selling a discounted room instead of a full priced one has to be measured in order to make the best decision. Thus, when a customer approaches the hotel for a discounted price, the manager needs to evaluate this scenario with the expected revenue from another customer who might come at a later date, willing to pay a higher price for the same room. The manager would accept the request only if the discounted price now is more than the expected price at which the room might be booked by the second customer. The key word here is "expected". RM systems use complicated mathematical algorithms to arrive at this decision using techniques such as Littlewoods and Expectation Maximization, referred to as the EM algorithm.

To explain these techniques, let us consider a simple two class scenario. A hotel has two price categories of rooms, say \$60 and \$100. Since the pricing is different for the two rooms, these rooms are each targeted at a different customer set. Based on the historical preference pattern of customers in each segment, it would be possible to estimate the number of customers who would be willing to buy these rooms at the given price, with a reasonable "variance". The term variance refers to a tolerance level. For example, an average 50 customers may be willing to pay \$100 for some rooms, but it could also mean that the actual number of customers who turn up for the \$100 room could be 60 (or even 40) with some probability, or 80 (or 30) with a lesser probability. In statistical terms, this sort of pattern for the different customer segments is said to mimic a normal distribution.

Using the past data and applying statistical know-how, we can actually estimate an "expectation" of revenue by quantifying the probability of a specific demand value and the actual revenue. In the same example, let us assume that this hotel has 100 rooms, which are similar, but priced at the time of booking. If the booking is done fairly closely to the actual date of stay, the customers may need to pay \$100, whereas, they might have paid only \$60 had they booked in advance. Remember that, on an average, 50 persons are willing to pay $100 for this room. Obviously, many more than 50 (say, 120) are willing to $60 for the same room. We can use the Littlewoods rule to actually estimate the number of rooms that must be protected for those customers who are willing to pay $100. If we protect too many rooms, some rooms may go vacant thereby resulting in a loss of potential revenue of at least $60 per room. On the other hand if we protect too few rooms for $100 customers, we lose the opportunity of $40 per room on that number of rooms. The Littlewoods rule guides us to arrive at an optimal number of rooms that would maximize the expectation of revenues.

Overbooking: Overbooking is the practice of intentionally selling more rooms than are available in order to offset the effect of cancellations and no-shows. Studies estimate that although a hotel is fully booked, about 5-8% of the rooms are vacant on any given date. Poor overbooking decisions can prove to be very expensive for the hotel. In the short run, it is only a loss of room revenue, but over the long-term, casualties may include decreased customer loyalty, loss of hotel reputation, etc. American Airlines developed an optimization model that maximizes net revenues associated with overbooking decisions for the airline industry.

To illustrate the overbooking model developed by the American Airlines, let us consider a B757 jet flying from Chicago to Boston. The aircraft has about 180 seats. Based on the past travel pattern, it is observed that an average of 5% (or nine passengers) do not turn up at the time of boarding the flight. If the airlines book all seats for this leg, it is likely to fly with only 171 occupied seats. However it does not mean that it never flies with 172 or more (even 180) seats occupied. There is a lesser chance of the flight flying with 172 passengers, an even lesser chance of it flying with 175 and a miniscule chance of it flying with all 180 passengers. Therefore, if we book 181 passengers instead of 180, we are likely to end up with only 173 passengers (and almost always with lesser than 180 passengers). In an odd event of exactly

181 passengers reporting, the airline would need to bump one passenger. IATA has defined rules to compensate bumped passengers. If we can quantify all costs (including the cost of lost goodwill), the expected revenue would be the revenue from 181 passengers minus the expected cost of compensating the one additional passenger at that odd chance. Since the probability of exactly 181 passengers turning up is so low, the revenue from that additional passenger generally compensates more than the expected cost. For this example, the optimal number of passengers that can be booked would be 186 as illustrated in the figure below.

This model can be directly applied to the hotel industry as well. The driving force behind the model is the evaluation of the tradeoff between additional revenue accrued by selling an already-reserved room versus the downside from doing so. It has been found that net revenue increases with overbooking until the point where the downside from overbooking a room exceeds customer revenues. Beyond that point, the negative impact of overbooking increases rapidly because fewer and fewer customers appreciate being turned away.

CHALLENGES

It is quite clear that while an RM system can guarantee increased revenues, it can be quite complicated to design and requires high levels of expertise for implementation. Some of the challenges facing hotels in the implementation of a robust and accurate RM system include:

- Measuring performance of an RM system is a major issue. Occupancy rates and yield are measures that are affected by external competition. An ideal measurement can be done using an opportunity model that indicates where the hotel stands in comparison to its maximum and
- Differential pricing is here to stay-customers seem resigned to the fact that hotels charge different prices

for the same room. However, some customers do not like this practice and penalize the hotel by not becoming a patron. Therefore, in a fiercely competitive environment where quality of service is the key to success, RM may not work. In evaluating the efficiency of a RM system, the trade-off between generating short-term profits and creating long-term customer loyalty and "mindshare" needs to be studied carefully.

- From an operational point of view, RM can impact the motivational level of the employees. In many cases, RM takes much of the guess work out of employees, thereby reducing their decision-making responsibilities. Sometimes, employees taking reservations are paid a percentage of the sales they make, motivating them to make group bookings, which in turn may be contradictory with the objectives of an RM system.

CONCLUSION

As part of ongoing changes in the industry, companies throughout the entire hospitality spectrum are placing a strong emphasis on implementing major operational changes. Beyond recognizing that meaningful cost reductions must be achieved without compromising safety, capacity and service levels, they are also looking at reducing costs by increasing flexibility and improving asset utilization through an RM strategy. In doing so, they continue to reassess their true core competencies, and are looking to outsource many of these processes, as they look to optimize business efficiencies and increase profitability.

11

INDIAN TOURISM INDUSTRY

INTRODUCTION

India has significant potential for becoming a major global tourist destination. The country witnessed foreign tourist arrivals of 2.75 million in 2001.

* Travel and tourism is the second highest foreign exchange earner for India, and the government has given organisations in this industry export house status. The industry is waking up to the potential of domestic tourism as well, with an estimated 4.7 billion domestic trips in 2001. Tourism spending within India in 2001 was US$ 22 billion.
* There is considerable government presence in the travel and tourism industry. Each state has a tourism corporation, which typically runs a chain of hotels / motels and operates package tours, while the central government runs the India Tourism Development Corporation. Divestment of these state-run tourism corporations have either already taken place or are in process.
* Incoming foreign tourist arrivals have shown a 6% compounded annual growth rate over the last 10 years. The government has realised the potential and has advanced several incentives to promote infrastructure growth in the tourism sector.

* Current investments are likely to see hotel room capacity increase by 20% over the next three years, with several international hotel chains entering the hotel industry. Similar growth is anticipated in air travel capacity.

Policy Initiatives

* The New Tourism Policy released in May 2002 has outlined the following policy initiatives for the tourism sector:
* The new policy is built around the 7-S Mantra of Swaagat (welcome), Soochanaa (information), Suvidhaa (facilitation), Surakshaa (security), Sahyog (cooperation), Sanrachnaa (infrastructure) and Safaai (cleanliness).
* The new policy envisages making tourism a catalyst in employment generation, wealth creation, development of remote and rural areas, environment preservation and social integration. The policy also aims to spruce up economic growth and promote India's strengths as a tourism destination that is both safe and at the same time exciting.
* The policy proposes the inclusion of tourism in the concurrent list of the Constitution so as to enable both the central and state governments to participate in the development of the sector.
* No approval is required for foreign equity of up to 51 per cent in tourism projects. Enhanced equity is considered on a case-to-case basis. NRI investment is allowed up to 100%.
* Approvals for Technology agreements in the hotel industry are available on an automatic basis, subject to the fulfilment of certain specified parameters.
* Concession rates on customs duty of 25% for goods that are required for initial setting up, or for substantial expansion of hotels.

* 50% of profits derived by hotels, travel agents and tour operators in foreign exchange are exempt from income tax. The remaining profits are also exempt if reinvested in a tourism related project.
* Approved hotels are entitled to import essential goods relating to the hotel and tourism industry up to the value of 25% of the foreign exchange earned by them in the preceding licensing year. This limit for approved travel agents/tour operators is 10%.
* Hotels located in locations other than the four major metro cities are entitled to 30% deduction from profit, for a ten-year period.
* The expenditure tax has been waived in respect of hotels located in the hills, rural areas, places of pilgrimage or specified place of tourist importance.

THE NEW BOOM THAT'S SWEEPING INDIA

Boomtown Gurgaon has spends that step city New Delhi would envy, but it has (almost) no hotels--little wonder that the highest room rate realisation in the national capital region is in Gurgaon's Trident Hilton, beating its luxury counterparts ITC Maurya Sheraton, The Oberoi, Taj Mahal Hotel, Hyatt Regency in the capital by far.

The Trident is a first-class international hotel, a euphemism for a three-star hotel (even though this property is at par with most five-stars); the others are established five-star hotels that would rather be referred to as seven-star properties.

Hotel rooms are hard to come by in Mumbai, and rentals can be astronomical by most standards. But it is Bangalore's Leela Palace that is the most expensive business hotel in the country, and if you arrive in the city without a booking, be prepared to pay the rate du jour, a whimsical rate of the day that you'll be hard put to explain on your expense account.

With guests outnumbering hotel rooms, and demand spiralling far ahead of supply, is it any wonder that travellers feel hotels are being opportunistic, making money while they can?

And is it any wonder that the same hoteliers seem to be spending more time with real estate developers (to sign land or joint venture deals) than on their services?

When international chains that have traditionally ignored India can't get enough of its market, funding is no issue at all (in the seventies, banks treated hotels on par with films as a risk venture), and the hotel boom could have a significant impact on India's total room capacity in the next couple of years.

Some numbers. In 2005, 3.92 million foreign tourists (this term includes business travellers) visited India, while the availability of "approved" hotel rooms was a mere 1,00,000.

For the ninth and tenth five-year plans, the Ministry of Tourism's official projection of hotel rooms is pegged at a conservative 1,25,000 (for an estimated 3.5 million foreign tourists a year). Indian travellers have not been factored in.

But with international air capacity into India increasing by leaps and bounds, and its markets pointing the future for companies and countries across the globe, get ready to be grounded unless the great room rush takes off.

But creating more rooms isn't the ministry's priority, and K B Kachru, executive vice president, South Asia, for Carlson Hotels (think Radisson), feels that the current gap, in spite of the building boom, will continue well beyond 2009-' and even then, the demand supply mismatch will remain over 50 per cent.

Markets like Mumbai, Hyderabad, Bangalore and Chennai are buzzing. Chains can't seem to get enough rooms even in the same city. ITC, with two hotels in Chennai, is adding a third there.

The Oberoi group wants a third hotel in Delhi and is building a second one in Gurgaon (right next to its Trident brand). The Shangri-La, a recent entrant into the Indian market, is entering Bangalore with not one but three hotels.

Bharat Hotels' Lalit Suri (of the Grand chain) has staked out the under-construction 320-room, seven-star hotelfrom Balaji Hotels and Enterprises in Chennai.

Foreign player Accor has just about completed the 280-odd room Novotel in Hyderabad, Marriott commissioned a hotel in Chennai earlier this year, and will add Bangalore next month. It also has hotels coming up in Noida and Gurgaon. ITC subsidiary Fortune is staking out cities like Ludhiana, Siliguri and Vijawada in its current phase of growth.

The mall hysteria that had seized the real estate industry till recently seems to have transferred that delirium to hotels now.

And Mumbai offers ample reflection of this. Its hospitality market is booming with ITC, Trident, Ibis, Park Plaza, Sofitel, Four Seasons and Taj all set to start new hotels.

While the Oberoi Group's third hotel is coming up in the Bandra-Kurla complex, the Park group is actively looking at Navi Mumbai (and has begun work on a 300-room hotel in Hyderabad).

Four Seasons and Mandarin Oriental are both said to be part of the Mumbai rush, expected to last, according to analysts, for at least another five years.

According to a recent study by hotel monitoring body HVS International-India, while Hyderabad, Mumbai, Goa, Chennai, the NCR and Bangalore occupy top slot for hotels, emerging markets for the hotel industry include Pune, Cochin, Chandigarh, Ahmedabad and Vishakapatnam.

According to HVS data, while Hyderabad will need 8,000 rooms by 2009, supply will be more than 5,400 rooms. In

Goa, demand by 2009 will be as high as 6,500 rooms, but supply will not cross 2,800 rooms.

In Chennai, the projected demand at 7,500 rooms will far outstrip supply at 5,000, and in Bangalore, while demand will be anywhere between 14,000-20,000 rooms, supply will not be more than 6,800 rooms.

"This is certainly boom time in terms of construction and investment in hotels in India," says Andrew Quinlan, general manager, Shangri-La, New Delhi, whose chain is targetting 8-10 hotels by 2010. Quilan has a point: This is the first time since 1995-96 that the hotel industry is experiencing growth of such magnitude.

And this time, the buzz around the entry of foreign players just won't go away. This is contrary to any developments--so far. HVS analysts say money for the new hotels is coming through equity, debt and FDI. Private placement and joint ventures are playing a major role.

So far, FDI in the sector seems to be coming in through real estate buyouts rather than in hotel projects.

Mandeep Lamba, managing director, Dawnay Day India, says that though there's a lot of talk about foreign companies entering the market, no serious commitments have been made yet.

"Dawnay Day, with an initial $200 million investment, is probably the only player which has made its intentions clear," says Lamba. It plans 30 three-to four-star hotels in the next three to five years.

Certainly, there's talk of Starwood Hotels (which owns the Sheraton, Westin and Meridien brands) scouting around Gurgaon for a property it hopes will help it leapfrog into ownership and management control in India.

With Accor's first Novotel ready in Hyderabad, the company is working on its projects in Gurgaon, Bangalore and Pune. And Sofitel has firmed up plans for Mumbai.

Carlson's K B Kachru says there are currently 26 hotels at various stages of development under the Carlson brands.

Eventually, though, it isn't a fight between foreign or homegrown chains as much as it is a struggle for marketshares.

The more the spread, the bigger the bite, and so Bharat Hotels "is definitely looking at offering 3,000 more rooms with plans for hotels in Chennai, Chandigarh, Jaipur, Noida, Hyderabad, Amritsar and other key locations by 2009," says Lalit Suri, chairman and managing director.

Riding on a wave of unprecedented room rate realisations, even summer occupancies continue to run high, upsetting the refurbishment plans of some city hotels traditionally taken up in the lean season.

Kapil Chopra, general manager, Trident Hilton, Gurgaon, says: "The hotel experienced an average occupancy of 91 per cent in May with an average room rate of Rs 11,800, a record price premium."

But what's the justification for their runaway rates? "It's all part of a business cycle," says Priya Paul, President, Park Hotels. "Don't forget that during a downturn we also reduce prices in order to keep the occupancy high."

Umesh Saraf, managing director, Unison Hotels, which owns The Grand (not to be confused with Lalit Suri's The Grand Intercontinental), adds: "Even at an average price of $250, Indian hotels are much cheaper than five-star hotels in the rest of the world that charge upwards of $400, and luxury hotels that charge over $550. In Paris, you will not get anything for less than □500."

All hoteliers say Delhi and Mumbai are world-class cities today, so there's no reason this should not be reflected in their hotel tariffs. They also say that business travellers are not complaining about the price.

While they're justfying hikes with add-on services, it would appear to make sense that hotel chains diversify their portfolios into a segment where there is a yawning gap--' mid-segment hotels.

But most hoteliers feel the economies do not support these, since the hotel-building industry in India is capital intensive. It's the reason Saraf is putting Rs 1,000 crore into hotel projects in Mumbai, Bangalore and the NCR--' all of them five-star.

Yet, mid-chain and even budget hotels have at least a few takers going for them. Accor, for instance, which has 4,500 economy hotels across the globe, or the Taj group's IndiOne that has morphed into the recently launched Ginger brand.

Ginger hotels (currently in Bangalore and Hardwar) is slated to launch a property every six weeks, and offer wi-fi systems, chic furniture, plasma TV, a tea kettle in the room and interntional toileteries at sub-Rs 1,000 rates.

"Its strategy? To get into areas that are cheaper and don't have competition. Launches are expected in Pimri (Pune), at IT Park in Trivandrum, and in Bhubaneswar and Mysore next.

Delhi-based InterGlobe Hotels, a joint venture between InterGlobe Enterprises and Accor Asia Pacific, plans to build 25 hotels under the brand Ibis in 12 years, five of which are already under execution. "Ranging between 150-215 rooms, Ibis hotels will focus on emerging cities like Gurgaon, Jaipur, Ludhiana and Jallandhar," says Uttam Dave, president and CEO, InterGlobe Hotels.

Others in the mid-segment are Sarovar, Easy Group, Country Inns & Suites and Indo-Asia Tours, the last set to have four-star properties with three-star tariffs (Rs 2,000-2,500) in tourist incentive destinations like Jaipur, Jodhpur, Coorg and Hampi.

On the other hand, Sarovar's no-frills Hometel hotels are commissioning in business locations Hyderabad, Pune, Mumbai and Chennai, and in newer destinations like Pushkar, Indore, Udaipur, Mussoorie and Baddi.

The logic is simple: with low-cost airlines, there is an inflow of budget tourists seeking rooms at more reasonable prices. The Rs 1,800 crore (Rs 18 billion) mid-hotel segment is expected to burgeon to Rs 4,600 crore (Rs 46 billion) by 2010.

At the opposite end of the spectrum are the Vilas hotels that belong to the Oberoi group, and which continue to win awards around the world for their service.

According to the company, the Rajvilas in Jaipur has had an extended high season till April. "It experienced almost 70 per cent occupancy against less than 60 per cent during the same month last year. Again, the Oberoi Amarvilas in Agra experienced a 15 per cent increase in occupancy since April last year," says a company spokesperson, reflecting the emerging importance of the leisure segment.

But with hoteliers and real estate developers all abuzz with hotel projects, is everything hunky dory in the land of pampering hospitality? Apparently not. Most in the industry crib about soaring land prices and getting the right locations in the cities.

"Land availability is a pre-requisite for a hotel to create room capacity. As most of the unencumbered land in cities is owned by the government, the Hotel Association of India (HAI) has taken on the task of trying to persuade state governments to consider creating land banks for ensuring availability of land at appropriate locations at reasonable prices," says Priya Paul, president of HAI.

Limitation to floor surface index (FSI) or floor area ratio (FAR) is another reason hoteliers cannot expand beyond a certain limit.

For instance, in Delhi and Mumbai, the FAR is between 1.25 and 1.75 (overseas, it can range between 5-15). With high land cost, especially in the central business districts (CBDs), there is a strong case for raising FAR limits, feel hoteliers.

According to Dave, the government will see serious bidders only when rates are reasonable. "Sometime back, the Delhi Development Authority had two to three rounds of auctions of properties in Delhi, but because the rates were so crazy, there were no takers," he says.

This is when the Commonwealth Games are round the corner, and also when Ministry of Tourism figures suggest that over 300 million Indians travel every year.

For the record, Delhi Development Authority auctioned four hotel plots for Rs 465 crore (Rs 4.65 billion) on June 6, soon after it had hauled in Rs 746 crore (Rs 7.46 billion) at another auction in March. The sites are all big plots and will in all likelihood be developed as five-star hotels.

Two of plots were bagged by Mumbai-based Asrani Inns & Resorts for Rs 127 crore (Rs 1.27 billion) and Rs 102.4 crore (Rs 1.024 billion) respectively. The DDA also managed to sell two other hotel sites at the Mayur Vihar District Centre for Rs 118 crore (Rs 1.18 billion) each. However, it could not find any takers for three sites at Shalimar Bagh, Shastri Park and Paschim Vihar.

There are many other issues that will dog the industry in the years to come, not least of which will be a severe manpower crunch. Which is why these figures might just be the jolt in the arm the government needs to take cognizance of an industry in its prime.

According to analysts, at its current strength the five-star hotel industry in India has a turnover of Rs 4,300 crore (Rs 43 billion). Add to this the mid-segment of Rs 1,850 crore (Rs 18.50 billion), which makes a total of Rs 6,150 crore (Rs 61.50 billion) (a large chunk of it in foreign exchange).

This means that growing at an annual 8.5 per cent, hotels will earn Rs 7,855 crore (Rs 78.55 billion) in another three years.

THE BOOMING TOURISM INDUSTRY

The year 2004-05 saw tourism emerging as one of the major sectors for growth of Indian economy, the foreign exchange earnings increased from Rs. 16,429 crore to 21,828 crore up to December.

Similarly in the last year, tourism industry registered a growth rate of 17.3% in foreign tourist arrivals, which has been the highest in last 10 years. Foreign exchange earnings grew at an even higher rate 30.2%.

India's tourism industry is thriving due to an increase in foreign tourists arrivals and greater than before travel by Indians to domestic and abroad destinations. The visitors are pouring in from all over the world: Europe, Africa, Southeast Asia and Australia. At the same time, the number of Indians travelling has also increased. Some tourists come from Middle East countries to witness the drenching monsoon rains in India, a phenomenon never seen in desert climates.

Domestic tourists are also fueling the industry's revival. Many of them escape from the summer heat on the plains to resorts in the Himalayan Mountains. One of the major beneficiaries this year is Kashmir, where a cease-fire between India and Pakistan has reduced violence, if not completely, at least enough to help revive the state's sagging tourism industry.

Among the most favoured tourist destinations in India, Kerala for its scenic beauty, Agra for Taj Mahal, Khujraho for its sculptures and temples, Goa for its beaches and some pilgrimages are the most important.

Interesting feature of this growth is that it has come even as global tourism has dropped, due to the September 11 terrorist attacks in the United States, the outbreak of

Severe Acute Respiratory Syndrome in East Asia, and the Iraq war. Even the disastrous tsunami didn't affect India's tourism industry, as tourist arrivals in India rose 23.5 percent in Dec 2004 and tourist arrivals crossed 3 million mark for the first time in 2004.

The disaster was expected to have a negative impact on India's tourism in terms of large-scale cancellations of tourists to India but nothing of that sort was seen.

REASONS FOR THIS BOOM

There could be several reasons for the buoyancy in the Indian tourism industry. First, the upward trend observed in the growth rate of Indian economy has raised middle class incomes, prompting more people to spend money on vacations abroad or at home.

Also, India is booming in the information technology industry and has become the IT center. Aggressive advertising campaign " Incredible India" by the government has also had contribution in changing India's image from that of a land of snake charmers, and sparking new interest among overseas travellers.

Tourism Contribution to the Indian Economy

It is not hidden that tourism is among India's important export industries. Even with comparatively low levels of international tourist traffic, tourism has already emerged as an important segment of the Indian economy.

Tourism also contributed to the economy indirectly through its linkages with other sectors like horticulture, agriculture, poultry, handicrafts and construction.

Foreign exchange earnings from tourism during 2003-04 were US $ 3,533 million (Rs 16,429 crore).

Besides being an important foreign exchange earner, tourism industry also provides employment to millions of people in India both directly and indirectly (through its linkage with other sectors of the economy.) It is estimated that total direct employment in the tourism sector is around 20 million.

Measures taken for Tourism Promotion

Recently, Indian government adopted a multi-pronged approach for promotion of tourism, which includes new mechanism for speedy implementation of tourism projects, development of integrated tourism circuits and rural destinations, special capacity building in the unorganized hospitality sector and new marketing strategy.

A nation wide campaign, for creating awareness about the effects of tourism and preservation of our rich heritage & culture, cleanliness and warm hospitality through a process of training and orientation was launched during 2004-05. The aim was to rebuild that sense of responsibility towards tourists among Indians and re-enforces the confidence of foreign tourist towards India as a preferred holiday destination. More than 6500 taxi drivers, restaurant owners and guides trained under the programme.

Government also took several other initiatives to promote Indian tourism industry and increased the plan allocation for tourism i.e. from Rs 325 crore in 2003-04 to Rs. 500 crore in 2004-05. Road shows in key source markets of Europe, Incredible India campaign on prominent TV channels and in magazines across the world were among the few steps taken to advertise Indian tourism. In addition a task force was set up to promote India as prominent health tourism destination.

However, in order to attract more visitors, India still needs to upgrade its airports, roads and other infrastructure to global standards. Even with the recent surge, tourist arrivals are just a mere percentage of those in such popular Asian destinations like Bangkok and Thailand.

RECENT DEVELOPMENTS

India Tourism office at Tokyo won two International Awards in Tour Expo held at Daegu in Korea for excellent tourism promotion. Indian Pavilion won the Best Booth Design Award as well as Best Folklore Performance Award competing with major players in tourism such as China, Japan, Thailand, Malaysia and Canada.

The theme of pavilion was the Buddhist pilgrimage in India. Multi promotional activities undertaken by Tokyo office drew a large crowd to India Pavilion, which added colours to the entire travel show.

The Korea's leading newspapers published on the front page the Incredible India booth's photographs highlighting various aspects. The live Yoga performance and Indian traditional snacks at the pavilion were enjoyed very much by the visitors.

This "Indian Tourism Industry Forecast (2007-2011)" report provides an objective analysis of the present scenario and future prospects of the Indian tourism industry. This report focuses on different parameters of tourism industry including: inbound tourism, outbound tourism, expenditure by inbound tourists, and medical tourism in India. It also helps clients to analyze the opportunities and factors critical to the success of tourism industry in India.

Key Findings

- In India, inbound tourist expenditure per head is third highest in the world and even more than global average tourist spending.
- India has been promoting its healthcare tourism by providing the visitors with private healthcare facilities. It is expected that the number of tourists visiting India for the purpose of medical treatment will reach one Million by 2012, representing a CAGR of 28.09% from 2007.

- Disposable income in past (during 2001-2006) grew at a CAGR of 10.11%, thereby driving domestic as well as outbound tourism.
- Room rent accounts for more than 50% of revenue earned by Indian hotel industry.
- Indian outbound tourist flow is expected to increase at a CAGR of 12.79% over the five-year period spanning 2007-2011.
- Tourist influx to India is expected to increase at a CAGR of 22.65% between 2007 and 2011.
- India's share in global tourism is expected to reach 1.5% by 2010.

Key Issues and Facts Analyzed

- What is the current state of tourism industry in India?
- What are the emerging trends in the tourism sector in India?
- What is the future outlook of the tourism industry in India in terms of inbound as well as outbound tourism, and expenditure by inbound and outbound tourists?
- Which factors are driving the India tourism industry?
- Hotel industry scenario in India?
- Hotel industry occupancy rate and room supply by 2011?

Key Players Analyzed

This section covers the key facts about the major players (tour operator & hotels) currently operating in the Indian tourism industry. The key players analyzed in this section include: Thomas Cook India Pvt. Ltd., Kuoni India Ltd., Cox & Kings India Ltd., Raj Travels & Tours Ltd., prominent Hotels & Resorts such as Taj Hotels, The Oberoi Group, Hyatt Corporation, ITC Welcomgroup.

Research Methodology Used

Information Sources: Information has been sourced from books, newspapers, trade journals, white papers, industry portals, government agencies, trade associations, by monitoring industry news and developments, and through access to access to more than 3000 paid databases.

Analysis Methods: The analysis methods include the following: Ratio Analysis, Historical Trend Analysis, Linear Regression Analysis using software tools, Judgmental Forecasting and Cause and Effect Analysis.

HOTELS IN INDIA-TRENDS AND OPPORTUNITY

Introduction

The scope of this publication is to assess current trends and future opportunities for the hotel industry in India. As always, apart from conducting specific research for this publication, we have included macro data provided by the Department of Tourism.

The publication briefly discusses the tourism industry in India in the context of the current economic scenario and presents the results of our survey on the performance of branded hotels, analysed by each segment of the hotel market, as well as by major cities. Our study also provides an overview of supply and demand conditions in the hotel market in India. As in previous editions of this report, we have, once again, presented our assessment of industry trends and developments; this is included as part of the 'Future Trends' section.

In addition to the Hotels in India-Trends and Opportunities we publish The Indian Hotel Industry Survey on an annual basis, in association with the Federation of Hotel & Restaurant Associations of India (FHRAI). This publication, the only one of its kind in India, provides detailed financial and operating information on the hotel industry, analysed by star category, across all major cities in the country. The 2003/04 edition will be available by the end of the year.

This is the eight edition of HVS International's Hotels in India-Trends and Opportunities publication. This year, 211 hotels, having a total room count of 28,870 rooms, participated in our research. The survey does not take into account any of the ITDC hotels, resulting in a decline in the total number of participating hotels (compared to 2003). However, overall room count has increased, reflecting the opening of new hotels with large inventories.

The Indian Economy-An Overview

The economy performed extremely well during 2003/04, with GDP growing by 8.2%. While agriculture accounted for most of the rebound (registering a growth of 9.1%, in response to the best monsoon in a decade), other sectors also showed a strong performance. Industry grew at above 7.0%. Services, which account for more than half of total GDP, expanded 8.7%. A key component of Services-the trade, financial services, hotels, insurance, transport and communications component-expanded by a seven-year high of 11.2% amid a credit-fuelled consumer spending spree.

The economy's buoyancy, together with initiatives by the erstwhile NDA government-to improve India's deficient infrastructure, divest loss-making enterprises and ease restrictions on foreign investment, and perhaps most importantly, make peace with neighbouring Pakistan-did much to convince the world of India's investment worthiness. More than $10 billion in foreign capital poured into India in 2003/04. However, this sense of bullishness has been somewhat dampened, following the NDA government's failure to return to power in the General Elections in April-May 2004, despite having done well in state elections last year.

The present Congress-led United Progressive Alliance (UPA) government's efforts to `open up' the economy (for example, raising FDI limits in telecom, aviation and insurance, which was proposed in the recently announced Union Budget 2004-05) are being thwarted by its main ally, the Left government. There are essential ideological differences between the two main parties: the Congress is progressive in outlook and both Prime Minister Singh and Finance Minister Chidambaram have been champions of reform; the Left, on the other hand, is not in favour of liberalisation and disinvestment. This has led to a sense of uncertainty as to the course government policy will take, causing foreign investors to hold back, and wait and watch, at least for the time being.

The Reserve Bank of India and leading research agencies have forecast a GDP growth of 6.0-6.5% in 2004/05, taking into account the likely adverse effects on agriculture of a late and erratic monsoon. However, recent data on first quarter (April-June) performance reveals the economy has, in fact, done better than expected. GDP growth for the period April-June 2004 is 7.4%. Agricultural production witnessed higher-than-expected 3.4% increase. Manufacturing grew at 8.0% during this period, exceeding the strong growth momentum witnessed in 2003/04. Demand for manufactured goods has, and will continue to, benefit from low interest rates, inexpensive and easily available financing options, and an overall rise in the purchasing power of India's population, over the last number of years. The trade, financial services, hotels, insurance, transport and communications component, which accounts for 50% of the Services sector, registered an 11.0% increase. Services and Industry will continue to drive the economy in the current fiscal.

Also in the economy's favour is its health: the balance of payments position is stable, a current account surplus is forecast for 2004/05 and India's foreign exchange reserves (US$118 billion as on September) are amongst the highest in the world. Moreover, the finance minister has strongly emphasised the government's commitment to liberalisation and key reform initiatives, assuring that they will be implemented, `even if there is a delay'. The government is also contemplating using a part of the foreign exchange reserves (say US$10 billion) towards major infrastructure development. The new government has been concerned about inflation, which has been rising steadily over the past three months, and touched a four-year high of 8.0% (in August-September). The increase is the result of seasonal factors and the higher prices of fuels and manufactured goods.

Trends and Developments in Tourism:

The year 2003 was an outstanding year in terms of inbound tourism, with tourist arrivals reaching 2.73 million. The strong growth in tourist arrivals in 2003 (especially in the first half of the year) is partly attributable to the outbreak of SARS in east Asia, as well as the war on Iraq, which resulted in India being perceived as a safe region to visit. The more fundamental reason, however, relates to a strong sense of business and investment confidence in India: inspired by India's strong GDP performance, and initiatives taken by the erstwhile Prime Minister, to make peace with Pakistan, strengthen ties with the developed world and open sectors of the economy to private sector/foreign investment. Significantly, the bulk of international arrivals in India, both in 2003 and 2004, have been business travellers.

Domestic travel, both business and leisure, also benefited from a thriving economy. Prior to being voted out of power, the NDA government implemented certain important measures to provide a much-needed boost to travel & tourism. These included the abolishment of the inland air travel tax of 15%; reduction in excise duty on aviation turbine fuel to 8%; and removal of a number of restrictions on outbound chartered flights, including those relating to frequency and size of aircraft. The provision included allowing Indian charters to land at all airports in the country, and Indian passport holders to travel on inbound charters. The government also launched the Incredible India campaign, which has been successful in launching the `Brand India' image.

The new government, it appears, is taking active interest in developing tourism in India. The continued Incredible India campaign has had a strongly positive impact on tourist arrivals in 2004. Definite efforts are being made to communicate the Brand India message: India made its presence strongly felt at the WTTC-promoted Global Travel & Tourism Summit held in Doha, Qatar in May this year. India has also been selected (on the basis of competitive bidding) to host the Summit next year.

An important new development is the government's recent decision to treat convention centres as part of core infrastructure, allowing the government to provide critical funding for the large capital investment that may be required. The government has identified Delhi, Mumbai and Goa as the markets to develop these convention centers, which is likely to further fuel demand for hotel rooms. Another effort is the decision to substantially upgrade 28 regional airports in smaller towns, slated to be completed by 2006. Expressions of interest have been received for the proposed privatisation (49% stake) of the Delhi and Mumbai international airports, but, as expected, the Left government has opposed the move.

Substantial investments in tourism infrastructure are, undoubtedly, essential for this industry to continue to evolve and grow, and ultimately achieve its potential. The upgrading of national highways connecting various parts of India has opened new avenues for the development of budget hotels alongside. Taking advantage of this and certain other key locations is the Tata group (owners of Indian Hotel-Taj) that has developed IndiOne, a 101-room economy hotel outside Bangalore; they hope to duplicate this across India in the next few years. Another hotel chain called `Homotel', being promoted by Sarovar Park Plaza group is also likely to compete in this new economy segment. International majors like Accor are also planning to bring in Ibis into India.

The year 2004 has been a record year in tourist arrivals, as is evident from data on foreign arrivals for the first eight months of the year. According to provisional estimates of the Ministry of Tourism, January to August 2004 saw approximately 2,093,600 visitors to India, 25.8% more than in the corresponding period of 2003. Growth has been spurred by large increases in airline passenger capacity: international airlines have added more than 4,000 seats a week on international routes to India in the last six months alone.

Increases in passenger capacity will play a significant role in fuelling growth in travel & tourism. British Airways has recently been permitted to triple its flights to India, and carriers from Australia are now allowed to offer 4,500 seats a week to India, more than double existing capacity. Moreover, Indian private carriers have recently commenced flights to the SAARC region, and have asked the government to be permitted to fly to East Asian countries. Capacity increases will not only bring in more international arrivals, but will, over a period, reduce airline fares to India, which are currently amongst the highest in the world.

Assuming a stable economic and political climate worldwide, the outlook for inbound tourism-both business and leisure-is strongly encouraging. Many international investors, particularly those who have invested heavily into China in the past few years, are now looking at India as the next opportunity. Conde Nast Traveller, in its readers' travel awards for 2004, has placed India at number six among the world's tourist destinations.

Domestic tourism will continue to develop rapidly and, according to HVS, will be the real driving force for this industry over the next decade or so. This segment will be helped by the growing wealth base of India's population and discounted fare options. A significant new development is the arrival of low-cost carriers, pioneered in India by Air Deccan, with other industry players such as Air India (short-haul, all-economy flights to the Middle East and Southeast

Asia) and Indian Airlines readying themselves to enter the low-cost market.

According to recent estimates of the WTTC, Indian tourism will grow at 8.8 per cent over the next 10 years, which would place India among the most rapidly growing tourism markets in the world. A longer term, sustained growth of the industry depends on how successfully several issues are addressed-relating to old and poorly facilitated airports, inadequate hotels, poor road and transport infrastructure, high levels of taxation and a bureaucratic visa processing system. As of now, at least, India is clearly taking steps in the right direction.

Hotel Supply

In the recent past, we have been asked several times about the actual supply of hotel rooms in India. Taking into account all approved and un-approved hotels, we estimate this figure to be close to 90,000 rooms. This is an abysmal figure for a country of India's size and population. An increase in business sentiments, leading to higher business-related travel or increase in foreign tourist arrivals, causes occupancy in markets to go up dramatically.

The year 2003, as we all know, showed an especially strong performance of the tourism industry. While there has been much talk about foreign arrivals, very little has actually been said about domestic tourism, which has grown by about 40% in the last four to five years. Government statistics point to approximately 230 million domestic travellers in 2002 and indicate that this number has risen between 15-20% in 2003. Domestic tourism has, in fact, been the staple diet on which a number of domestic leisure destinations have sustained themselves-the hotel markets of Goa, Jaipur, Agra and various hill stations being among these. With disposable incomes having risen significantly in the last five to seven years, across much of India's middle income and upper-middle income segments, families have been taking more holidays-and spending more on their vacations-than ever before. The concept of travelling for leisure has, in recent years, gained a more widespread appeal, not only with families, but also young adults, a segment that is earning far more than their parents did at that age. With a certain degree of social change taking place across India, domestic tourism is poised to grow rapidly in the coming years.

The Development of Branded Hotels in Major Indian Cities

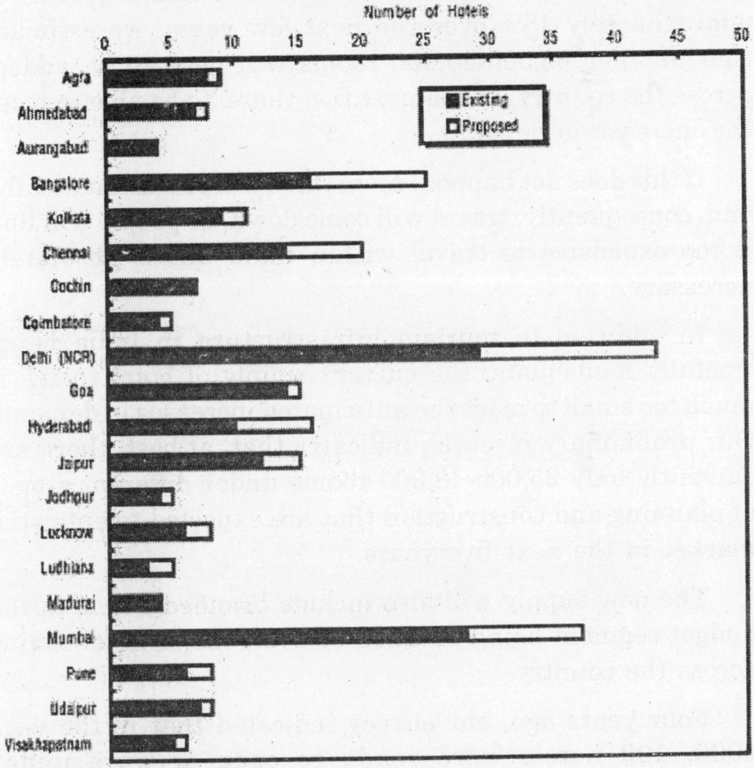

Source: HVS International Reseach

When will India actually touch the 'magic number' of 5 million tourist arrivals? This is a question that those involved in travel & tourism, or the hospitality industry, often ask. This year, for the first time ever, India is going to cross the three million mark. According to our estimates, India would witness nearly 3.5 million foreign tourist arrivals in 2004. The sharp rise in arrivals-as well as the increase in domestic travel-is already showing in the high occupancies of hotels across various cities.

Demand for room nights grew at approximately 18% across the country in 2003/04 (according to HVS estimates) and is growing at 15-20% in the current fiscal.

Taking into account an estimated demand growth of approximately 18% over the next few years, we estimate that another 65,000-80,000 rooms will need to be added, across the country, in the next five years, to be able to meet the increase in demand.

If this does not happen, room rates will rise dramatically, and, consequently, travel will come down, as people will find it too expensive to travel within India unless absolutely necessary.

In addition to tourism infrastructure in India being woefully inadequate, the current supply of hotel rooms is much too small to meet the anticipated increases in demand. Our preliminary research indicates that, at best, there are currently only 35,000-40,000 rooms under different stages of planning and construction that are expected to enter the market in the next five years.

The new supply will also include branded hotels in the budget segment being planned by some major hotel chains across the country.

Four years ago, our survey indicated that in the year 2000, 109 hotels were ready to open or were under construction. Last year, this number (hotels expected to open in the next few years) had declined to 63. This year, the number of new hotels under development has once again risen to 97. Moreover, as per our assumptions, an additional 100 economy hotels will also be developed in the economy segment. The maximum development is likely to be witnessed in the National Capital Region (NCR), particularly in Gurgaon. Bangalore and Mumbai are next in line, where at least 9-10 projects are currently under consideration. Hyderabad and Chennai are also likely to witness 5-6 new hotels. We expect the new economy hotels to be developed mostly in secondary and tertiary locations.

With regard to the expected increase in supply, it is entirely possible that a number of these projects will face financial difficulties while in progress. The blame for this lies with both the government agencies as well as the new developers. A classic example is that of the numerous developments in Gurgaon.

The local government is auctioning land for commercial development (including hotels) at high prices, thus forcing new developers (bid winners) to build hotels that are luxury or upper mid-market in orientation, whereas the need of the hour is budget hotels or dedicated extended stay products. Many of the new developers do not want to be seen building budget hotels, as this does not fit in with the profile of their other businesses.

Thus, several such developers are tending to partner with operators who are desperate to enter a particular market and will compromise their standards for location / partner and product just to plant a flag. The recent success of some hotels in Gurgaon-which have done extremely well and beyond most expectations-has been the main motivator for these businessmen.

These new owners, it seems, have failed to realize that when 7-9 hotels open at the same time (in the next three to four years), only those projects that have been careful planned and executed will survive the competition or the next phase of economic slowdown in the country.

The NCR still remains the favourite destination, in terms of the number of new hotels slated to become operational in the next few years. Seventeen hotels are in various stages of planning and development in the NCR, of which eleven properties are expected to be located in Gurgaon. We understand that, apart from these, there may be a few additional properties under development in West Delhi as well.

Survey Results

The HVS International survey has been computed by dividing the respondent branded hotels into their respective classifications according to star grading. As before, we have examined the performance of ten major cities across India, wherever a reasonable sample allowed. While most of the responses to the survey were given in Indian Rupees, we have presented some results in US Dollars as well.

For the first time in six years, both occupancy and average room rates improved in 2003/04. The performance in US Dollar terms was even better due to the appreciation of the Indian Rupee. The number of budget hotels in the branded segment in India has increased significantly over the past several years, and today represents approximately 35% of the total rooms in our survey. The increased representation of branded budget hotels has lowered the overall industry figure for average rate. However, it may be noted that, over a five-year period, the compounded growth has been the strongest in the budget segment. The RevPAR of the three-star hotel segment grew at 10.9%, followed by four-star at 8.7%. The slowest growth was, in fact, witnessed in the five-star deluxe segment, which grew marginally, at 1.2%.

For the second time in a row, there has been an across-the-board improvement in occupancy: average occupancy rose by 12.6% in 2003/04, compared to 10.9% the previous year. Demand for hotel room nights improved across all-star categories in 2003/04, with occupancy close to or higher than double digits, in each segment. The five-star category has witnessed the most growth (16.7%), followed by four-star (15.2%). The increase in occupancy levels this year was even stronger than in the previous year. In terms of average rate, all star categories experienced healthy growth in 2003/04. The four-star segment experienced the most improvement (10.1%), while the five-star segment witnessed the least improvement (5.7%). In US Dollar terms the four-star segment grew at 15.4%, followed by three-star (12.1%) and five-star deluxe (12.0%).

Average rate in Rupee terms increased at 8.3% (compared to a 5.7% decline in 2002/03), resulting in an overall improvement of 21.9% in RevPAR or a 27.6% RevPAR increase in US Dollar terms. Average rate in US Dollar terms showed a countrywide increase of, 13.4%.

Hotel Occupancy Rate for Ten Key Cities in India, Between 1999/2000 and 2003/04

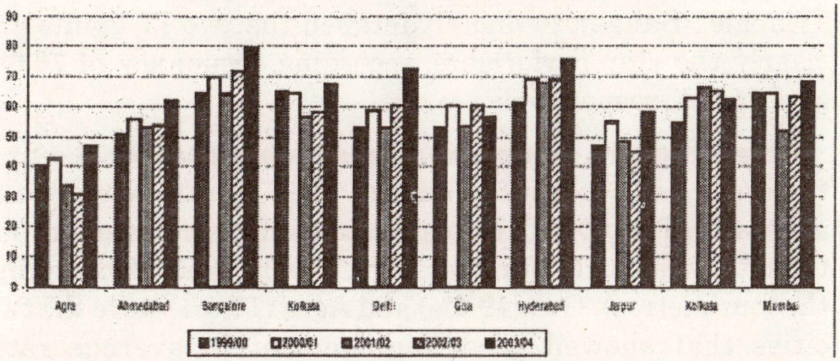

Average Rates for the Hotels in Each of these Cities, Expressed in Rupees

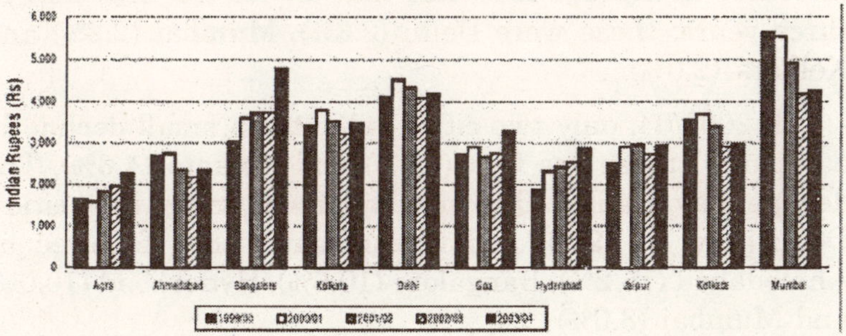

Corresponding RevPAR Data for Each City, in Rupees

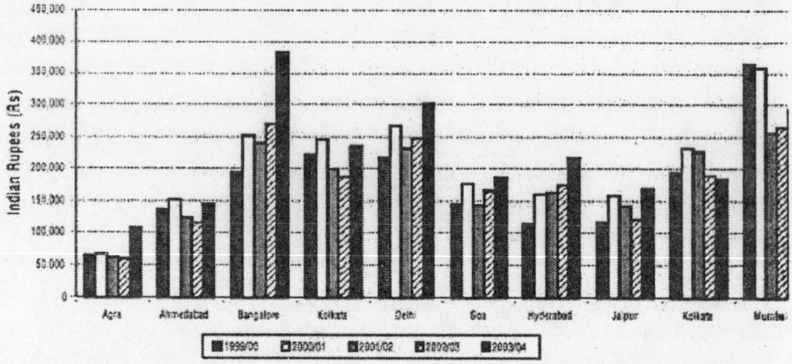

A new and interesting trend is that Agra and Jaipur have seen substantial improvement in their performance in terms of occupancy, growing at 53.1% and 29.8%, respectively. This is followed by Delhi, which is part of the 'Golden Triangle'. Bangalore and Hyderabad-the two IT giants-are clearly the star performers, recording occupancy of 79.6% and 75.8%, respectively.

Significantly, Bangalore displaces Mumbai for the first time and has become the market average rate leader with a growth of 28.0%. This is an astonishing achievement for the city which, till four years ago, was ranked fifth (behind the four metros). Goa (19.6%) and Agra (17.0%) were the two cities that showed good improvement in average rate. Hyderabad, which has generally been a very price sensitive market, also grew at 12.8%. Three large metros had modest increases in average rate, and that too for the first time in three years: these were Delhi (2.3%), Mumbai (2.2%) and Kolkata (2.0%).

In 2003/04, only two cities exhibited a small decline in occupancy: these are Goa (6.3%) and Kolkata (4.6%). The decline may attributed to new supply entering these cities. Delhi grew at 19.9% and Chennai at 15.8%, followed by Ahmedabad (15.2%), Bangalore (10.6%), Hyderabad (10.0%) and Mumbai (8.0%).

In terms of RevPAR in 2003/04, Bangalore was in number one position, followed by Delhi, Mumbai and Chennai, with Mumbai having been relegated to third place for the first time. However, the biggest improvement during 2003/04 in terms of RevPAR was seen in Agra (79.1%), followed by Bangalore (41.5%) and Jaipur (39.1%). The only decline in RevPAR was seen in Kolkata (2.7%).

All cities, with the exception of Mumbai and Kolkata, have experienced positive improvement in terms of compounded growth of RevPAR. Over a five-year compounded period, the two main centres of IT activity-Bangalore (18.3%) and Hyderabad (17.4%)-have grown the most. Negative growth was witnessed in Mumbai (-5.4%) and Kolkata (-1.2%) over the same period. This is much to do with a situation of oversupply in these markets.

The year 2003/04 saw significant supply additions to several cities, with the maximum growth witnessed in Goa, Mumbai and Kolkata. A huge surge in demand in Goa and North Mumbai has helped in absorbing this new supply. Goa may have experienced decline in occupancy, but its overall performance, in light of the supply increase, is commendable. With very little new supply expected in Bangalore, Hyderabad and Goa over the next two years, we expect these markets to improve significantly. In addition, in the medium term, even Delhi, Mumbai and Chennai are likely to improve. Average rates in cities like Bangalore and Hyderabad are likely to be substantially higher, with Bangalore registering among the strongest growth worldwide. In the leisure segment, we expect Jaipur to see a slowdown, however, Goa remains a very strong prospect.

Future Trends

HVS has been conducting this survey for seven years, and, for, the first time, it appears that Indian hotel industry has completed a full cycle, experiencing both downswing and upswing periods. The industry is robust at present, and there are clear indications are that the next two to three years will be even stronger. Certain markets are already seeing huge un-accommodated demand during weekdays, with average rates in some of these markets witnessing unprecedented increases. All the ten cities we studied have seen a positive trend in both occupancy and average rate.

While all cities have seen increases in rooms occupied per day (over the previous year's corresponding period), Goa (28.7%) is the market leader, this is what has allowed this leisure destination to absorb the new supply increase of 23.8%. Mumbai (18.1%) has the second highest growth. In fact, of the seven cities studied by us, Hyderabad was the only city to have a single-digit growth (9.4%). Chennai (17.9%) Bangalore (15.9%), New Delhi (12.9%) were the other strong performers in the market.

In terms of average rate, Bangalore (58.4%), Hyderabad (21.2%), New Delhi (9.7%) and Chennai (9.2%) have all had increases. In fact Kolkata is the only market which saw average rates decline marginally. Year-to-date occupancy for Bangalore at 80% means that there is not much potential for further increase in occupancy, as weekdays are mostly sold out. Strongly escalating demand has caused hotels to push rates way beyond what they should be getting for the quality of product they offer. This is certainly true of some of the properties that never had a proper refurbishment and are now charging exorbitant rates.

We would expect operators to raise average rates strongly in Hyderabad as well. Recent indications are that the hotels in south Mumbai have also started to see improvements in performance. This effectively means that Mumbai is poised to see good growth in terms of both occupancy and room rate increases as demand outpaces supply. Goa and Delhi are also expected to see some rate increases. Traditionally, average rates rise in October, therefore, our data is not reflective of rate increases that are likely to take place shortly. Many of these rates are negotiated rates with corporates and travel agents which will come into effect as the peak season kicks in.

The most encouraging development during the first five months of the current year has been the healthy increase in RevPAR across all cities. Bangalore (61.2%), followed by Hyderabad (32.6%), have, for the second time in a row, witnessed the highest growth in terms of RevPAR. Chennai (27.4%), Goa (23.0%) and New Delhi (12.2%) have seen double-digit growths. Mumbai (9.9%) and Kolkata (9.5%) also witnessed single digit growth.

The Goa market has performed exceptionally well and in the years to come will be one of the best performing markets. The city over the past two years has seen substantial increases in rooms supply, despite this demand continues to outstrip supply, resulting in occupancies to go up marginally even in the current year. At present there is not much new hotel activity planned for Goa, making this one of the preferred location for investment. Another market performing extremely well (but is not part of this survey) is the Pune market.

The sharp upturn in Bangalore's performance is beyond what most hotel owners and developers had anticipated. Despite HVS having forecast the city's hotel market to do a sharp turnaround we, too, are taken by surprise by the extent of improvement. Existing hotel owners can expect a windfall gain this year as well as for the next few years, until new supply enters the market. The Leela Bangalore is amongst the biggest beneficiaries; this hotel is already setting records for highest average rates in the country for a business hotel (US$275-US$300). We understand that at least 9 hotels are planning to enter Bangalore. As a result, we can expect the market to slow down in two to three years with rates declining sharply.

The trends witnessed in Delhi in 2004 have been quite positive, reinforcing our faith in the city. Occupancies have picked up over the past few months, especially in hotels closer to Gurgaon. These hotels enjoy much healthier occupancies than city centre hotels which, in fact, are pulling down overall occupancy levels. Year-to-date average rate growth is only 3.2%, but is anticipated to increase further during the peak season. Also, with the proposed conversion of Kanishka to Shangri la and Ashok Yatri Nivas' re-development, we can expect further competition within Delhi's central business areas. The new Trident Hilton (in Gurgaon) has been an extremely good performer and is currently market leader in terms of RevPAR.

Opportunities

Opportunities for the Indian hotel sector continue to be in the budget and mid-market segment: we anticipate these segments to witness huge growth and expansion, in the next year or two. The luxury segment is set to perform extremely well over the next few years until the supply-demand gap is bridged.

We expect average rates to grow in all major cities across India. New opportunities lie in the extended stay segment, which many potential developers are currently shying away from. Also, HVS has observed that owners interested in developing extended stay properties are keen to partner with existing branded chains already operating in India. This, according to us, is an area where specialized serviced apartment chains like Oakwood and Ascot have tremendous scope for involvement. This is particularly true in destinations that are near large concentrations of IT and related services development.

Medical tourism could also be the next big thing, and, while we are yet to see any development in this area, we consider that there could be some potential. If world class convention centres are indeed developed in Mumbai, Delhi and Goa (as proposed, with government support), these cities are sure to benefit. Similarly the further liberalization of the aviation sector would mean additional tourists, and with supply unable to keep pace with demand, nearly all segments of the hotel industry would see improvement.

HVS is of the view that if you are not already building a hotel in India, then you are late. The present period of upswing however, we believe, will last longer than the previous period of upturn (1995-97). There are clear indications that travel & tourism in India will grow faster now than ever before this bodes well for the hotel industry.

In last year's edition of this report, we mentioned that Agra and Jaipur were the weak links in the industry. Thanks to increase in both inbound and domestic tourism, the two cities have experienced the strongest recovery over the 12-month period. We expect this trend to persist into the current year as tourist arrivals continue to go up. Agra, while having seen highest improvement, has still a long way to go (citywide occupancy 47%). There also some unfinished hotel projects in Agra, which will continue to put pressure on the city's performance. As regards Jaipur, the recent announcement by a major IT company to set up a base outside Jaipur, as well as the state government's initiative to promote IT-related activity in the city, means that Jaipur can look forward to some additional room night demand from the business segment. These developments in the leisure segment including the strong performance in Goa leads us to believe that the leisure segment is clearly benefiting from the increase in foreign tourist arrivals and growth in domestic travel. We also consider that in the future years new leisure destinations in Kerela and other coastal areas will also pick up. Recent announcements by the Government of India to promote tourism in the Andaman and Nicobar Islands could not therefore have come at a better time.

Hotels in metro cities, with an average rate of Rs 2,600-3,000, and hotels in non-metro cities, with an average rate of Rs 1,800-2,400, are likely to experience rapid growth in demand in the next year or two. Cities to watch out for, in terms of development opportunity, are Pune, Goa, and certain pockets in major cities like Delhi (west) and Mumbai (mill lands). We would however, like to caution investors to stay away from the current 'hotspots' of Hyderabad, Bangalore and Gurgaon, as large additions to supply have been planned here. The real opportunity, we believe, is in a good mid-market or budget hotel of international standards.

TOURISM OF INDIA-STAR HOTELS IN INDIA

Like most of the countries in world, India also has hotels divided in different categories depending on their location, facilities, infrastructure, and amenities provided. All the star hotels in India are government approved with continuous control on the quality of services offered.

Five Star Deluxe Hotels

The most luxurious and conveniently located hotels in India are grouped under Five Star Deluxe Hotel Category. Five Star Deluxe hotels in India are globally competitive in the quality of service provided, facilities offered, and accommodation options. These hotels are located primarily in metropolitan cities like New Delhi and Mumbai and major tourist destinations like Jaipur, Agra, and Goa.

Five Star Hotels

These are top of the line hotels located mostly in the big cities. These hotels provide all the modern facilities for accommodation and recreation matching international standards in hospitality. Many of these hotels are situated in the Central Business Districts of the metropolitan cities or near the centers of transportation providing exceptional value for the business travellers.

Four Star Hotels

A rung below five star hotels, these hotels provide all the modern amenities to the travellers with a limited budget.

Quality of the services is almost as high as the five stars and above categories. These kind of hotels are there for the travellers with a limited budget or for the places which might not getting the tourist traffic associated with larger cities.

Three Star Hotels

These are mainly economy class hotels located in the bigger and smaller cities and catering to the needs of budget travellers. Lesser in amenities and facilities, these hotels are value for money and gives good accommodation and related services on the reduced price. Services would be the stripped down version of higher categories of hotels but sufficient to fulfill your basic needs.

Two Star Hotels

These hotels are most available in the small cities and in particular areas of larger cities. Catering to the backpacker tourist traffic, these hotels provide all the basic facilities needed for general accommodation and offers lowest prices.

One Star Hotels

The hotels with most basic facilities, small number of rooms, and location in the far flung areas are grouped under One Star Hotel category. These hotels are best when you are looking for cheapest available accommodation option (apart from camps and hostels).

Heritage Hotels

Heritage hotels in India are best if you are looking for sheer elegance, luxury, and royal treatment. They are not just another accommodation options but tourist attractions in themselves. Exquisitely designed and decorated, meticulously preserved, high standards of service, and ethnic cultural motifs helps the tourists get the complete experience of an India that otherwise exists only in the history books.

Beach Resorts Hotels

Peninsular India bounded by Arabian Sea, Bay of Bengal, Indian Ocean and the two emerald archipelagos of Lakshwadeep and Andaman and Nicobar have a long coastline of around 7500 km, offering an amazing array of beaches, some popular, some not so well known.

Wildlife Resorts Hotels

A wildlife tour is incomplete if you don't actually live in a forest for a few days. Imagine living in a rest house or a tent the midst of the dense wilderness, and waking up to the twittering of birds, or maybe the roar of a lion! Day trips alone are certainly not enough to show you the true majesty of the wild, so why not try this too?

Government Approved Hotels

These are the hotels, which might not have applied for star categorization or small enough to find them in the list. Many of the wildlife resorts, lodges, and hostels are government approved providing a minimum level of accommodation facilities at far off places.

Action Plan

To elevate tourism as the economic and employment priority.

Long Term

Department of Tourism will function as the nodal agency in co-ordinating all the activities related to tourism being undertaken by different sectors of economy under different names; To develop mechanisms to protect the tourism industry from the adverse effects of multilateral agreements, like GATTS, WTO Agreements etc.; Include Tourism in the school & college curriculum to create awareness among youths.

Medium Term

Encourage studies on potential of tourism sector compared to other sectors of economy in the state; Conduct scientific studies on the inter-sectoral issues affecting the development of tourism.

Short Term

To have an Apex body with Chief Minister as Chairman, and Ministers and Secretaries of Tourism, Forest, Irrigation, Power, Revenue, Public Works, Local Self Government, Industry, Finance, Culture, Transport, Fisheries, IT, Health, Science & Technology, Vice Chairman State Planning Board, Director Tourism, and 4 nominated tourism experts as members to discuss and decide the inter-sectoral issues in development of tourism; Conduct scientific studies on impact of tourism on income and employment through Tourism Satellite Accounting; Strengthen the collection of statistics on tourist arrivals, tourist profile, expenditure pattern etc.; Conduct awareness campaign through local bodies, District Tourism Promotion Councils clubs & social organisations; Prepare short films on the benefits of tourism and broadcast in visual media and at prominent places such as railway stations; To pursue sustainable tourism development with focus on Conservation and Preservation of Heritag.

Long Term

Assess Carrying capacity of all the tourist centres to regulate the developments accordingly.

Establish systems and procedures to enforce and include core components of sustainable tourism development vis a vis conservation, preservation and benefit sharing with local communities/people.

Medium Terms

Prepare Area development plans for all the tourism destinations and to regulate the developments accordingly;

Plans and implementation to be reviewed and suitably modified periodically.

Short Term

Enact Tourism Conservation, Preservation and Trade Act to guide & regulate the tourism growth & development;

Identify Special Tourism Zones and enforce the Act to regulate developments and to conserve the heritage;

Encourage Industry Associations to impose regulations on the industry on their own for preventing unethical or illegal activity;

Take up Studies on carrying capacity assessment for all the major destinations;

Involve the community in the planning, awareness building and benefits sharing from the tourism projects and implementation stages of all the projects;

Make environmental impact assessment for all the major projects as a pre-requisite for sanction.

To Guarantee Quality Services in all Sectors of Tourism

Long Term

Allow only approved tourism units by Department of Tourism to function as tourism units in the State;

Medium Term

Encourage units to upgrade quality. Improve enforcement of exiting legislation for this by various departments;

Short Term

Enforce legislation for the approval of tourism units such as accommodation, restaurant, tour operation, tourist transport operation, ayurveda centres, houseboats, recreation centres, cultural centres, tourism sports, amusements parks, Home Stays, amusement traveller etc. as a symbol of quality;

Ensure only approved units will find place in the publicity material published by Department of Tourism and be eligible for incentives offered by Department of Tourism from time to time;

Inculcate a spirit of service among functionaries concerned with tourism.

To Create and Develop Infrastructure through Private Sector

Long Term

Ensure withdrawal of Government from direct running of all the tourism business activities;

Withdraw all financial incentives to private sector investment and encourage the sector to invest in more open and competitive environment;

Medium Term

Try joint venture with major hotel chains within the country both in private and public sectors;

Ensure regular meeting of the Apex Body under the chairmanship of Chief Minister to address any issue related to provisions and basic infrastructure facilities to tourism units;

Short Term

Introduce Single window systems for clearing tourism projects;

Encourage private investors to avail loans from financial institutions such as SIDBI, KSIDC etc in large-scale infrastructure projects;

Establish separate cell in financial institutions like KSIDC and KFC for tourism with representatives from Tourism for the speedy clearance of tourism related projects. Simplify the procedure for sanctions;

Launch Special campaigns for NRI and foreign investments in tourism sector;

Encourage the investors to take up projects to establish connectivity between tourist destinations within the State by air and road;

Encourage development of products such as golf, shopping facilities, marina, amusement & recreational parks etc.;

Use land bank scheme operated by Tourist Resorts (Kerala) Ltd. to acquire potential land for tourism development and for attracting private investment;

Encourage small businesses to serve tourists through internet access centres, free telecommunication services, tourist information centres, local transportation agencies and hygienic food joints.

INCENTIVES OFFERED TO PRIVATE SECTOR INVESTMENTS

Investment Subsidy

General investment subsidy of 10% of capital cost including land, building, furniture, furnishings, equipment, landscaping etc. subject to a maximum of Rs.10.00 lakhs will continue for approved tourism units. Additional subsidy on the following will also be provided;

a) Investment in pollution control facilities and equipments such as solid/liquid waste management equipments for recycling of wastewater, sanitation facilities, captive power generation (generators) etc @ 15% of such investments subject to a separate ceiling of Rs.5.00 lakhs.

b) Projects with capital investment exceeding Rs.50.00 crores may be considered for a special incentive package except tax-based incentives, not below the benefits otherwise eligible, on a case-to-case basis.

c) Special package of incentives will be considered for channelising Foreign Director Investment (FDI) in tourism and infrastructure projects.

Electricity Tariff Concession

The existing system of remitting the commercial tariff and getting the difference of commercial tariff and industrial tariff from Department of Tourism will continue.

CONTINUE FOCUS ON BACKWATERS, AYURVEDA AND ECO-TOURISM

Long Term

Backwaters: Link the waterways from Kovalam to Kasargod to enable operation of tourist boats including houseboats;

Develop necessary infrastructure all along the backwater such as boat terminals, jetties, wayside facilities, fuel-pumping stations, sewage pumping stations etc;

Inter link all the major nodes along the backwaters with the road networks to enable easy transits;

Initiate measures to enhance the quality of ecology and environment of backwaters;

Establish proper solid and liquid waste management system for backwater.

Ayurveda

Allow only approved ayurveda centres by Department of Tourism and Health Department to function at tourism centres in the name of tourism;

Educate tourists about genuine Ayurveda;

Eco-Tourism

To develop a chain of forest lodges across the various sanctuaries of the State by converting unused or under-used

Inspection Bungalows, Inspection quarters and other buildings of the Forest Department;

Evolve a clear cut strategy to co-ordinate all Department and private sector who are having eco-tourism recourses and provide synergy for the development of the same;

Market eco-tourism products of Kerala in the international scenario as a distinct product;

Prepare a monitoring mechanism for eco-tourism products;

Develop Zero waste Zones in and around tourist destinations;

Develop and promote non-conventional use of energy;

Constitute eco-development committee in tourism areas.

Medium Term

Backwater

Regulate activities along the entire backwater, canal and lake stretches with respect to setbacks from the water front, design of the buildings, solid waste and sewage disposal etc.;

Formulate Backwater Tourism Development Authority with representatives from all stakeholders exclusively to co-ordinate the infrastructural development activities for the sustainable use of the backwaters for tourism purposes;

Stop discharging the sewage directly to the water by any boat used for tourism purpose by enforcing usage of alternative methods.

Ayurveda

Constitute a committee with members from Department of Tourism, Directorate of Indian System of Medicine, and tourism industry to constantly review the implications in using Ayurveda as a tourism product.

Eco Tourism

Evolve strategies to attract private investment in eco-tourism products; Evolve strategies to empower local people to benefit from the emerging economic opportunities;

Evolve special efforts to tap the eco-tourism potential of the Forest Department, which can ultimately lead to conservation of the resources.

Create eco-tourism centres in backwaters, Wayanad, Idukki, Kasargode and Kannur District; Develop Plantation Tourism involving public sector enterprises, Oil Palm India Ltd., and Rehabilitation Plantation Ltd., which falls in the region of Thenmala eco-tourism;

Develop the concept of rural tourism;

Short Term

Backwater

Construct basic tourism facilities such as boat terminals and waterside facility centres along the houseboat cruise routes from Kollam to Ernakulam;

Disperse backwater based tourism activities to Malabar Region by developing infrastructure at potential centres such as Chettuva, Kadalundi, Kozhikode, Parassinikkadavu, Neeleswaram, Valiyaparamba etc.;

Prepare a master plan for the sustainable use of the backwaters of Kerala for tourism purposes;

Institute special annual award for the most innovative backwater based tourism product;

Encourage quality upgradation of the houseboats through incentives;

Ayurveda

Strengthen the approval system and bring in classification system to grade the ayurveda centres based on the quality of facilities and services;

Eco Tourism

Identify and develop atleast 25 special trek routes and promote in a strictly controlled way. Tourism Department/ Forest Department may do the management of the customer interface;

Start Elephant rides at 3 or 4 sanctuaries;

Formulate specific eco-tourism strategy for Kerala through participatory planning process;

Completion of the ongoing works related to eco-friendly general tourism at Thenmala and surroundings;

Establish the Environment Education centres in the State;

Initiate eco-tourism programme at Konni and Achankovil;

Develop and promote Eco and wild safari activities in sanctuaries;

To Concentrate on Development of Basic Infrastructure and New Tourism Products

Long Term

Develop direct air connections from all major tourism markets to all the 3 international airports;

Develop all the major tourism roads on P.V.P. basis;

Ensure adequate water supply, sewage, drainage and solid & liquid waste disposal system in all tourist centres;

Medium Term

Co-ordinate with other States, with Government of India and with international tourism bodies like WTO, WTTC and financial bodies like UNDP, World Bank, ADB etc. for seeking assistance in tourism development;

Develop new cruise circuits connecting major Ports in South India and neighbouring countries such as Sri Lanka, Maldives and Mauritius;

Prepare Master Plans for identifying and creating additional tourist areas comprising of religious sites, beach/backwater resorts, business destinations etc.;

Short Term

Prepare a project report by identifying all major tourist roads and pose it for external financial assistance in collaboration with PWD;

Initiate basic infrastructure projects at the tourist destinations and get it done through other departments and agencies giving financial assistance, if needed or outsourcing;

Improve facilities at airports, sea ports and bus stations;

Focussed development of identified Special Tourism Areas/Zones; Develop inter-State tourism circuits connecting all destinations in South India;

Sites of well-known temples/places of worship to be developed and given sufficient publicity as religious sites for pilgrimage; Develop exclusive pilgrim circuits;

Develop quality maps for the entire State as well as for specific places of interest within it;

Install qualitatively excellent road tourism signages through out the State;

Encourage homestay scheme;

Use Kerala cuisine as an effective instrument for promotion of tourism;

Promote adventure tourism including water sports;

To Create Sufficient Quality Human Resources in the Field of Tourism within the State

Long Term

Open an Institution of international repute in the State to train quality managerial manpower to manage the tourism industry in the State;

Create the best-trained personnel in the tourism industry to cater to the needs both inside and outside the State;

Medium Term

Create a Board/Institution to regulate and approve the Institutions conducting tourism related courses;

Short Term

Strengthen KITTS to start new courses directly benefiting the tourism industry; Conduct continuous training programmes to train the various categories of people such as taxi drivers, cooks, waiters, guides, information offices/ assistants etc. engaged in the tourism industry; Encourage starting of new institutions with quality standards in private sector.

To Strengthen the Institutional Mechanism

Long Term

Professionalise the entire functions of Department of Tourism.

Medium Term

Separate the hospitality function from Tourism Department and form a separate Hospitality Department; Strengthen Planning, Marketing and Information wings of Department of Tourism by bringing more professionals into it; Stop District Tourism Promotion Councils from direct management of facilities. Identify new role for DTPCs in information dissemination, quality control and micro-level regulation.

Short Term

Enact new role for Department of Tourism to regulate the developments and ensure quality of products and services, marketing and information dissemination; Professionalise all the areas of tourism; Restructure Kerala Tourism Development Corporation.

To Develop and Promote Souvenir, Handicrafts, Artifacts and Shopping Industry

Long Term

Develop souvenir & handicrafts as important tourism products; Create the best-trained personnel in the souvenir, handicrafts, artifacts Field;

Medium Term

Organise shopping festivals for handicrafts and souvenirs with Kerala tastes; Standardise the quality of souvenir, handicrafts and handloom products and bring in a system of approval and classification.

Short Term

Engage a consultant (individual/agency) for the development of Souvenir industry in the state. The scope of work would include assessment of present scenario, design, quality and marketing; Identify new items & products in handicrafts, handloom & souvenir industry sector; Improve the design and skills of artisans; Agencies such as Kerala Handicrafts Development Corporation, Khadi Board, Kudumbasree, DTPCs, NGOs etc. will be involved in developing souvenir & handicrafts as important tourism products; Promote the products through suitable marketing strategies.

To Enact Proper Legislation to Sustain the Industry and to Regulate Tourism Activities

Long Term

Enact and enforce legislation for achieving this objective.

Medium Term

Revise the Excise law to distinguish between quality hotels providing liquor as a facility (bar attached with hotels) and normal bar where the hotel is attached to a bar to meet the legal requirements; Revise the laws on entertainment tax, luxury tax, sales tax, building tax etc. to incorporate provisions for encouraging investors; Enact and enforce proper building rules to ensure quality in hotels/resorts etc.; Include punitive measures to violator.

Short Term

Enact Tourism Conservation and Preservation Act to regulate the developments in the identified tourism zones and ensure quality services in all major sectors of the industry; Enact and enforce proper liquid and solid waste management systems for hospitality industry.

To Explore and Develop New Markets for Kerala Tourism Products at Domestic and International Markets

Long Term

Focus on domestic tourism, Asia and Gulf countries; Acknowledge the emerging economic super power status of China to attract more tourists; Market as an eco-tourism destination with strict guidelines to investors, visitors against mass tourism, human rights violation and bio-piracy.

Medium Term

Focus on Europe, US, Japan, China, Gulf and domestic markets; Make use of better political relation in the South Asian region to attract more regional tourists.

Short Term

Focus on Europe, US, Japan, Gulf and domestic markets; Continue and strengthen marketing in the high yielding markets mentioned above; Undertake promotional activities with the help of Central Government agencies such as Government of India Tourist Offices in India and abroad; Use Information Technology efficiently and effectively for the promotion of tourism; Persuade Government of India to revive the scheme of Leave Travel Concession.

To Conserve and Preserve the Cultural Heritage of the State

Long Term

Create a partnership with industry and NGOs to educate the public about the need to conserve and preserve the heritage and implement an action plan.

Medium Term

Work with INTACH, Art and Heritage Commission and Cultural institutions to synergise tourism and culture. Ensure culture is not degraded by commercialisation; Develop a Museum of Theyyam and other Folk Arts at North Kerala; Highlight the sites of unique activities in Kerala, like rubber tapping, todday tapping, Kerala's culture, Sabarimala, Guruvayoor, Jewish Synagogue at Cochin, the oldest Church, the oldest Mosque, Sites at Calicut where Vasco De Gama and Chinese Admirals landed etc.

Short Term

Introduce legislation through appropriate departments to conserve and preserve cultural and heritage properties; Encourage promotion of local cultural programmes, folk arts, boat races etc.; Promote regular traditional cultural programmes in key destinations; Promote approval of institutions giving short-term course in performing arts of Kerala and give wide publicity; Promote a few colourful festivals intensively; Promote a few major tourist oriented traditional festivals in each district; Develop Heritage walkways in Thiruvananthapuram.

To Ensure Safety and Security of Tourists

Long Term

Strict legislation on ensuring the quality of all tourism products; Mechanism for speedy disposal of cases where tourists are involved.

Medium Term

Improve communication facilities at tourist destinations; Introduce insurance scheme to tourists; Ensure quality of all tourism products in terms of its safety conditions.

Short Term

Every brochure to contain the Do's and Don'ts for tourists; Deploy sufficient numbers of Tourist Polices (men and women) at major tourist destinations; Deploy sufficient numbers of lifeguards at beaches; Open a complaint and suggestion cell at Directorate of Tourism to handle the complaints from the tourists; Strengthen mechanism to discourage and prevent illegal activities by touts and middlemen who harass tourists.

GENERAL ECONOMIC SERVICES

Tourism

Tourism activities in Uttar Pradesh were formally initiated in the last year of the First Five Year Plan with a token provision of Rs. 1.00 lakh. This amount was utilised in the creation of wayside amenities to the tourists/pilgrims on yatra routes. Since then the department of Tourism has been continuously endeavouring to achieve greater heights. In view of the tourism potential available in the State, an independent Directorate was set up in the year 1972 for providing tourist facilities like accommodation, food etc., to the tourists. For commercial activities, a U.P. State Tourist Development Corporation was also set up in 1974 with an authorised capital of Rs. 100.00 lakh.

Performance During Ninth Five Year Plan

For the Ninth Five Year Plan 1997-2002, an outlay of Rs. 500.00 crore was earmarked for tourism sector in the State which included Rs. 400.00 crore to be spent on the development of second phase of Buddhist Circuit project. An outlay, therefore, of Rs. 100.00 crore was available for the works to be carried out in State and District Sectors. The amount of Rs. 400.00 crore earmarked specifically for the second phase of Buddhist Circuit project could not, however, be utilised for want of financial sanction from the Government of India. As regards other works, an yearwise break-up of outlay and expenditure is as follows:-

(Rs. in lakh)

Ninth Five Year Plan	Outlay	Expenditure
1997-98	4716.28	4265.61
1998-99	5000.00	3262.65
1999-2000	4446.36	644.94
2000-01	2424.48	1299.63
2001-02	3086.23	1871.32

Thus, a sum of about Rs. 113.00 crore was spent against the outlay of Rs. 100.00 crore in the Ninth Five Year Plan. Apart from this, 57 projects amounting to Rs.4.23 Cr. were also got sanctioned from the Government of India.

As a result of tourism promotion activities, nearly 830 lakh domestic and 8.48 lakh foreign tourists visited Uttar Pradesh in the year 2000-01 as against the target of 2271 lakh for domestic and 50 lakh for foreign tourists for Ninth plan period. However, in the first three years of Ninth Plan, nearly 2446 lakh domestic and 23 lakh foreign tourists have already visited places of tourist interest in U.P. It is estimated that the State contributes nearly 20% of the total foreign exchange earned by India. Number of foreign tourists who visited Uttar Pradesh during the last five years and the foreign exchange earned therefrom is as follows:

Year	No. of foreign Tourists (in lakh nos.)	
	In India	In U.P.
1998	23.59	7.27
1999	24.82	8.00
2000	26.41	8.48
2001	25.37	7.95
2002	23.84	7.10

Year	Foreign Exchange earned (in crore Rs.)	
	Total	U.P.'s share
1998	12150	2433
1999	12951	2590
2000	14475	2772
2001	14006	2661
2002	14195	2839

Apart from the above, income from the domestic tourists is also as under:-

Year	No. of domestic tourists (in lakh)	Income from domestic tourists (in crore Rs.)
1998	785.60	4560
1999	772.37	4801
2000	667.03	5069
2001	1447.88	11003
2002	714.90	5504

Tenth Five Year Plan

Aims and Objectives

Keeping in line with the international standards, facilities are planned to be created to ensure that the tourists to Uttar Pradesh should get physically invigorated, mentally rejuvenated, culturally enriched and spiritually elevated.

According to the strategy adopted for implementation of projects in the Tenth Five Year Plan, top priority is assigned to the completion of on-going works of previous plans to avoid further escalation in their cost. This will also help tourists to have benefits of these projects much earlier. Besides Paryatan Bhavan and provision of basic infrastructural facilities, State share for central schemes has also been given priority over others so that the component of central financial assistance to be released from the Government of India is not held up. The main objective of the Department of Tourism is to provide neat and clean accommodation, hygienic food, comfortable transport and healthy recreation to the tourists at various tourist places and make them aware of the rich historical and cultural legacy of the State. With this view, a tourism policy has been framed on the basis of tourist circuits in the State. Circuit-based development works as envisaged in this policy are aimed at integrated

Development of the area ensuring removal of regional imbalances and creation of job opportunities. The Department of Tourism has identified the following circuits to be developed for tourism promotion in the State.

- Buddhist Circuit
- Bundelkhand Circuit
- 3-Vindhya Circuit
- Braj (Agra-Mathura) Circuit
- Avadh Circuit
- Wild-life, Eco-tourism and Adventure Circuit
- Water Cruise Circuit

Basic infrastructural facilities like electricity, drinking, water, accommodation and transport are proposed to be provided on these identified circuits. It is also proposed to link all the circuits by rail, road, air and wherever necessary by cruise services so that the tourists could get easy access to their destinations. For this purpose, it would be desirable that a small amount of 5% of the total budget of the Lok Nirman Vibhag be specifically earmarked for those roads which are important from tourism point of view and could be spent on maintenance and upkeep of such roads as may be recommended by the Department of Tourism, U.P. All the works included in the Tenth Five Year Plan and which are associated with the identified circuits would be kept in State /Central sector. Prior studies are proposed to be done for each circuit separately for their integrated development. Two such Master Plans are have already been prepared for Buddhist and Bundelkhand Circuits. Studies of Kalinjar, Chitrakut and world heritage centre, Varanasi are proposed to be done through INTACH which has already done a study on Chunar as a Tourist Resort.

For the Tenth Five Year Plan 2002-07, a sum of Rs. 1382.73 Cr. was earmarked for tourism sector in Uttar Pradesh. Out of this amount, a sum of Rs. 1032.73 Cr. was for the externally aided projects alone. Thus only an amount of Rs. 350.00 Cr. is left for State and District Sector works. It is expected that nearly 31.88 Cr. would be spent in first two years of the five year plan period which is nearly 9% of the outlay left for the State and District Sector works.

As against the target of 1108 lakh Indian and 52 lakh foreign tourists in U.P. in five years, only 900 lakh domestic and 10 lakh foreign tourists are expected to be visiting U.P. by the end of the Tenth five year plan period. Number of foreign tourists has, however, declined due to terrorist activities around the world.

An outlay of Rs. 2500.00 lakh had been allotted for the year 2002-03 against which Rs. 1478.72 lakh had been spent. Similarly an outlay of Rs. 4000.00 lakh had been allotted for the year 2003-04 and Rs. 1209.37 had been spent against the outlay.

Annual Plan 2004-05

An outlay of Rs. 4103.36 lakh is proposed in tourism sector for the Annual Plan 2004-05. This outlay includes Rs. 1475.36 lakh in district sector and Rs. 2628.00 lakh in the State sector.

In view of the constraints of financial resources in the State, participation of private sector in tourism trade is contemplated in a big way. For this purpose, an attractive package of incentives to private investors is included in the tourism policy. The role of public sector would be restricted to a mere 'Promoter' providing only infrastructural facilities at the tourist spots.

Employment Generation

In the Tenth Five Year Plan, a sum of Rs. 1344.40 lakh was earmarked for construction works in tourism projects. It is expected that during the Five Year Plan period, an employment of about 950 lakh mandays would be generated in the construction phase. It is also estimated that nearly 5317 persons would be getting direct employment apart from those getting benefits indirectly through tourism projects.

12

PACKAGE HOLIDAY

INTRODUCTION

A package holiday or package tour consists of transport and accommodation advertised and sold together by a vendor known as a tour operator. Other services may be provided like a rental car, activities or outings during the holiday. Transport can be via charter airline to a foreign country. Package holidays are a form of product bundling.

Package holidays are organised by a tour operator and sold to a consumer by a travel agent. Some travel agents are employees of tour operators, others are independent.

Organised Tours

The first organised tours dated back to Thomas Cook who, on 5 July 1841, chartered a train to take a group of temperance campaigners from Leicester to a rally in Loughborough, twenty miles away. Thomas Cook-the company-grew to become one of the largest and most well known travel agents before being nationalised in 1948. With the gradual decline of visits to British seaside resorts after the Second World War, Thomas Cook began promoting foreign holidays (particularly Italy, Spain and Switzerland) in the early 1950s.

Information films were shown at town halls throughout Britain. However, they made a costly decision by not going into the new form of cheap holidays which combined the transport and accommodation arrangements into a single 'package'. The company went further into decline and were only rescued by a consortium buy-out on 26 May 1972

PACKAGE TOURS

Vladimir Raitz, the co-founder of the Horizon Holiday Group, pioneered the first mass package holidays abroad with charter flights between Gatwick airport and Corsica in 1950, and organised the first package holiday to Palma in 1952, Lourdes in 1953, and the Costa Brava and Sardinia in 1954. In addition, the amendments made in Montreal to the Convention on International Civil Aviation on June 14, 1954 was very liberal to Spain, allowing impetus for mass tourism using charter planes.

By the late 1950s and 1960s, these cheap package holidays-which combined flight, transfers and accommodation-provided the first chance for most people in the United Kingdom to have affordable travel abroad. One of the first charter airlines was Euravia, which commenced flights from Manchester Airport in 1961 and Luton Airport in 1962.

Despite opening up mass tourism to Crete and the Algarve in 1970, the package tour industry declined during the 1970s. On 15 August 1974, the industry was shaken when the second-largest tour operator, Court Line which operated under the brand names of Horizon and Clarksons, collapsed. Nearly 50,000 tourists were stranded overseas and a further 100,000 faced the loss of booking deposits.

Recently a growing number of consumers are avoiding package holidays and instead are travelling with budget airlines and booking their own accommodation. In the UK, the downturn in the package holiday market led to the consolidation of the tour operator market, which is now dominated by a few large tour operators. The major operators are Thomson Holidays, part of the TUI AG, Thomas Cook

AG, MyTravel, and First Choice. Under these umbrella brands there exists a whole range of different holiday operators catering to different markets, such as Club 18-30 or Simply Travel.

DYNAMIC PACKAGING

Dynamic Packaging is a method that is becoming increasingly used in package holiday booking procedures that enables consumers to build their own package of flights, accommodation and hire car instead of a pre-defined package.

Free Independent Traveller

Free Independent Traveler/Tourist (or FIT) refers to both a way of travelling and, from an industry viewpoint, a sector within the tourism market. FITs practise a form of Dynamic packaging but the emphasis is from the end-user point of view and includes the wider economic effects that FITs "spread" in their destination country as opposed to more traditional, consolidated forms of travel.

Bibliography

Abram, Simone: *Tourists and Tourism: Identifying with People and Places*, New York, Berg, 1997.

Andrew Holden: *Tourism: A New Perspective*, London, Prentice Hall, 1995.

Andronicou, Antonios: *Tourism in Cyprus*, New York, Oxford University Press, 1979.

Apostolopulos, Y., S. Lewadi: *The Sociology of Tourism*, New York, Routledge, 1996.

Ashworth, Gregory J.: *Marketing Tourism Places*, London, Routledge, 1990.

Bennett, O.: *Financing for Tourism Projects in Developing Countries*, England, Wiley, 1994.

Bevan, D. L., and D. W. Soskice: *Appraising Tourist Development in a Small Economy*, London, Heinemann, 1976.

Boissevain, Jeremy: *Coping with Tourists: European Reactions to Mass Tourism*, England, Berghahn, 1996.

Brogan, E.: *Human Resource Development in Tourism: The Scottish Perspective*, England, Wiley, 1994.

Bruce, David : *Tourism Strategies for Rural Development*, Sackville, New Brunswick, 1993.

Byran, H.: *In Tourism Alternatives: Potentials and Problems in the Development of Tourism*, Philadelphia, University of Pennsylvania Press, 1992.

Chambers, Erve: *Tourism and Culture: An Applied Perspective*, Albany, State University of New York Press, 1997.

Cooper, C.: *Tourism: Principles and Practice*, London, Pitman, 1993.

Creque, Darwin: *A Study of the Tourist Industry in the U.S. Virgin Islands*, North Carolina, Amalie, 1964.

Daniel, R.: *Recent Advances in Tourism Marketing Research*, New York, Hawthorne Press, 1996.

David, L.: *International Tourism Policy*, New York, Van Nostrand Reinhold, 1990.

David, W.: *Tourism Planning*, Chicago, Council of Planning Librarians, 1995.

Davidson, R.: *European Business Travel and Tourism*, England, Wiley, 1994.

Douglas, C.: *Heritage Tourism is in the Future of Many Alabama Communities*, Auburn Univ., Auburn, 1991.

Douglas, Pearce: *Change in Tourism: People, Places, Processes*, New York, Routledge, 1995.

Edward, M.: *In International Tourism: Identity and Change*, London, Sage, 1995.

Edward, M.: *In International Tourism: Identity and Change*, London, Sage, 1995.

Foley, M.: *In Tourism: The State of the Art*, England, Wiley, 1994.

Forbes, A. H.: *Tourism and Transport Policy in the European Union*, England, Wiley, 1994.

Frew, E.: *International Charter Travel—a New Opportunity for Australian Tourism*, England, Wiley, 1994.

Garfield, Donald: *Partners in Tourism: Culture and Commerce*, Washington, DC, American Association of Museums, 1997.

Gimblett, Barbara: *Destination Culture: Tourism, Museums, and Heritage*, California, University of California, 1998.

Gimblett, Barbara: *Destination Culture: Tourism, Museums, and Heritage*, California, University of California, 1998.

Gorman, Michael: *Design for Tourism: An ICSID Interdesign Report*, New York, Oxford University Press, 1972.

Harrison, David: *Tourism and the Less Developed Countries*, London, Belhaven, 1992.

Heise, Dorothy: *Promoting Tourism in Rural American*, Maryland, National Agriculture Library, 1991.

Hitchcock, Michael: *Tourism in South-East Asia*, London, Routledge, 1993.

Holden, Andrew: *Tourism: A Commodity of Opportunity for Change?* Chichester, England, 1994.

Howard Green: *Tourism and the Environment: A Sustainable Relationship*, New York, Routledge, 1995.

Huit, Groupe: *The Sociocultural Effects of Tourism in Tunisia: A Case Study of Sousse*. New York, Oxford University Press, 1979.

James Makens: *Marketing for Hospitality and Tourism*: New Jersey, Prentice-Hall, 1998.

Jenkins, C. L.: *Tourism in Developing Countries: The Privatisation Issue*, Chichester, England, 1994.

Jeremy, B.: *Coping with Tourists: European Reactions to Mass Tourism*, England, Berghahn, 1996.

John Sem: *A Training Guide for Rural Tourism Development*, Minnesota: Rural Tourism Center, 1995.

Knox, J.: *Tourism Research Priorities in Hawaii and the Pacific*, Honolulu, University of Hawaii, 1979.

Komilis, P.: *Tourism and Sustainable Regional Development*, Chichester, England, 1994.

Koth, Barbara: *A Training Guide for Rural Tourism Development*, Minnesota: Rural Tourism Center, 1995.

Kotler, Philip: *Marketing for Hospitality and Tourism*: New Jersey, Prentice-Hall, 1998.

Lawrence, R.: *Rural Tourist and Non-Tourist Communities in Massachusetts: Quality of Life Patterns*, 1980-1990, Pennsylvania, Northeastern Forest Experiment Station, 1993.

Lloyd, E.: *Tourism: A Shrinking World*, Columbus, Grid, 1980.

Martinus, J.: *Tourism by Train: Its Role in Alternative Tourism*, Philadelphia, University of Pennsylvania Press, 1992.

Mary, E.: *A Heritage Tourism Tool: National Register of Historic Places*, Radnor, Pennsylvania, 1993.

McConnell II, D. W.: *Nature-Based Tourism and Rural Coastal Development: Observations, Options, and Trends*, South Carolina, Clemson University, 1990.

Mieczkowski, Zbigniew: *Environmental Issues of Tourism and Recreation*, Lanham, University Press of America, 1995.

Muzaffer Uysal: *Recent Advances in Tourism Marketing Research*, New York, Hawthorne Press, 1996.

Muzaffer, Uysal: *Recent Advances in Tourism Marketing Research*, New York, Hawthorne Press, 1996.

Richard, W.: *Tourism and Recreation in Rural Areas*, Chichester, U.K., 1998.

Richard, W.: *Tourism and Recreation in Rural Areas*, Chichester, U.K., 1998.

Soskice, D.W.: *Appraising Tourist Development in a Small Economy*, London, Heinemann, 1976.

Stephen F.: *Linking Tourism, the Environment, and Sustainability*, Ogden, Utah, 1995.

Stephen, C.: *Tourism in the Navajo Country: Resources and Planning*, Winslow Rock, Navajo Tribe, 1967.

Valentine, Udoh: *Tourism Development: A Research Note on Africa*, Connecticut, Praeger, 1996.

William W. Swart: *Planning for Tourism Development: Quantitative Approaches*, New York, Praeger, 1976.

INDEX

L

M

N

O

P

R

S

T

❑❑❑